T0146925

Humbled Beginnings to Perfected Endings

"The Emerald Stone on the Top Shelf"

VIVIAN A. NESMITH, M.P.A.

WESTBOW
PRESS®
A DIVISION OF THOMAS NELSON
& ZONDERVAN

WestBow Press books may be ordered through booksellers or by contacting:

WestBow Press
A Division of Thomas Nelson & Zondervan
1663 Liberty Drive
Bloomington, IN 47403
www.westbowpress.com
844-714-3454

Scripture quotations are taken from the Holy Bible, King James Version.

ISBN: 979-8-3850-0888-9 (sc)
ISBN: 979-8-3850-0889-6 (hc)
ISBN: 979-8-3850-0890-2 (e)

Library of Congress Control Number: 2023918430

Print information available on the last page.

WestBow Press rev. date: 09/26/2023

This Book Belongs To:

_____

Acknowledgment

While sitting down, try admiring life accomplishments. Has the thought ever crossed your mind that Jesus Christ kept you through thick and thin? I hope so because every day is granted to us so we can receive His unmerited favor. I cannot imagine writing without the Holy Ghost for the last four books. My entire being exists because of Him, and I acknowledge Him in all I do. My testimonies reflect life experiences and the perils I went through to get to where Jesus Christ wants me to be. The task was not easy, and sometimes I felt like giving up, but I thought of all the times He kept me without thinking twice about it. Well, I say twice, based on my experience and feelings.

Folks dedicate books to their loved ones, friends, and family. "But, God!" He is the only LORD and SAVIOR who provides life and success and meets the necessities to live in this world. It is a world filled with sorrow, grief, and confusion. Hence, we are equipped to make something out of nothing—an impossible task for us but possible with God. So, we pick up the shattered, broken pieces of life, hand them over to Jesus Christ, and say, "Fix it, Jesus," and he makes us whole again.

From the depths of my soul, I look up, and with a sincere heart, I want to say unto The LORD: Thank you! You have brought my entire family and me through the storm, tempest winds, and pouring rains. Thank you, My Soul says thank you.

Contents

Searched For Emeralds

The Measure of Faith

Greener Things are a Mixture of Greens

What Color Are Your Leaves

Greenhouses

Genuine and Refurbished

The trial of our faith, being much more precious than of gold that perishes, though it be tried with fire, might be found unto praise, honor, and glory at the appearing of Jesus Christ.

The Only Way Now Is Up!

Introduction

Romans 10

Before reading this book, perform a self-check. Please use a pencil to mark your answer:

Did you accept Jesus Christ as Lord and Savior? **Yes or No**

If your answer is "**NO**" to the above question, "**STOP**," do not proceed to the next question! We can do this together—

Recite *Father, In the Name of Jesus, I confess with my mouth the Lord Jesus and believe in my heart that you have raised your Son Jesus Christ from the dead, and now I am saved.*

Now, answer the below questions.

1. Today, did you acknowledge Jesus Christ? **Yes or No**
2. Today, did you pray? **Yes or No**
3. Today, did you worship the LORD Jesus Christ? **Yes or No**
4. Did you read a chapter or more of the Word of God? **Yes or No**
5. Did you take notes? **Yes or No**

If the answer to any phrase is "NO!" I advise you to do so immediately. Your day will begin well, and with the Holy Ghost as your divine keeper, he will lead you through the day. If you feel you can go at it without the Armour of God, alone without another's help, then my brother or sister, you are aiming for failure. To understand life mishaps, you first need a covering shield; without it, you lack wisdom, knowledge, and understanding. Therefore, you are unable to handle the blows of life. What will happen is that the knees will buckle under the weight or burdens of the world. Then, it will crush your entire "person" because of pride.

Oh, I tricked you there for a minute. Listen, I write what the Holy Ghost gives me to write to the soul that needs it the most. I am not of excellent speech, the best writer; while reading this book, you will find many grammatical errors in punctuation and spelling. Yet, please do not judge this book by its cover or the person writing the words on every page. I do not proclaim to be any of the above. I proclaim to be a True Servant of God who speaks, preaches, and teaches according to His perfect will.

Listen, Friend, this book is about "Humbled Beginnings To Perfected Endings." The subtitle, "The Emerald Stone on the Top Shelf." As you read along with pages folded or wet, the Holy Ghost will enlighten your understanding, and you can evaluate if this book was resourceful. Ultimately, the most important thing is the relationship built with Jesus Christ. As a Saint of God, Servant of God, Child of God, Man or Woman of God, whatever title you desire, Jesus Christ is the main ingredient. So, repentance is in order, prayer and supplications keep communication lines open, and praise and worship are sweet melodies sung to The Father, personalized, written, and orchestrated by you.

Humbled beginnings define the "new you" fashioned in Jesus Christ. For others who have walked behind the LORD for many years, encountered bumps, bruises, or wounded on the battlefield, the Holy Ghost has humbled your experience. As you begin to evaluate a few things here and there, hopefully, the conclusion centers on the importance of building a relationship with Jesus Christ. Later, it transitions to "Perfected" endings because Jesus Christ is now in total control. You are the emerald stone on the top shelf, tried with fire, and have found praise, honor, and glory in and with Jesus Christ.

For our new brothers and sisters, the journey has just begun. Do not link yourself with another Saint of God to hold your hand along the way.

Food for the Soul—pick up your Bible; ask the Holy Ghost for wisdom, knowledge, and understanding before opening it. Then, please open it and start reading from Genesis and forward. Get into the habit of building your relationship with Jesus Christ alone by allowing Him the opportunity to enlighten and reveal himself to you. Furthermore, pray to the Lord, Jesus Christ, and ask Him to send you to a Church under

Pastoral leadership that feeds the flock of Jesus Christ according to sound doctrine that conforms to biblical truths. Also, pray the Shepherd would encourage growth in the talents given by the Holy Ghost. Finally, pray that when the time comes, they will teach you to spread your wings and fly, not clip them.

Listen, listen, listen—A devout Saint is intimidating to unrighteous Church Leadership. In fear and to cover their ineffectuality, they thwart your growth. You will not reach maturity if you fail to recognize your "Spiritual Growth" in the Body of Christ. We are to develop and produce good fruit. When a seed is planted, over time, it sprouts, and a transformation occurs. The seed does not remain a seed; it will wither and come to naught. Therefore, all Saints are to prosper in Christ.

You must fulfill your vacation and not remain bound to redundancy. Suppose you do not recognize your potential or answer the call to a higher vocation; you will wither and not produce good fruit. Remember, promotion comes from "The Lord," and no one has the power or authority to grant heavenly gifts. These treasures are bestowed upon the righteous from the Father. *James 1:17:* "Every good gift and every perfect gift is from above, and cometh down from the Father of lights, with whom is no variableness, neither shadow of turning."

Do not allow another to stunt your growth by diminishing your call.

Tried by The Fire

Growing up, we learned about the dangers of fire. If caught playing with matches, my mother lit a match and then asked us to touch the fire. She did this a few times to share the harmful effects it causes. Fire destroys and burns down houses; if our house burns down, we will have nowhere to go. So we were "home-trained" to never play with fire.

Sometimes, we are curious to determine what will result from our actions. If we are not attentive to instruction, it could be catastrophic for our future. Often, situations cause us to react in a way that is not pleasing to others and the LORD. Thus, he sends messengers and pricks our hearts to force us to focus on Him, not the problem. For a problem to exist, something or someone had to initiate it.

Complex trials sometimes cause us to doubt our position or relationship with Jesus Christ. So, you don't want to open your mouth about anything of the Word of God. Then, the Holy Ghost reminds you of everything you have experienced. At that moment, the Holy Ghost starts ministering to "your" inner man, and a conversation erupts, which causes tears to flow. Slowly, you lift your hand and give Jesus Christ a wave offering. Waving your hand is simply stating, "Yes, Lord! I hear your voice and receive the promise, whereas you will bring me out." It is easy to lose focus on the beautiful acts of mercy when intensely focusing on current situations.

Trials and tribulations will make you rethink who you are or who you are before you begin to lose sight of your purpose. If not 100 percent grounded in the Word of God, you will easily drift back into the world of deception. Looking at the situation becomes a distraction and decreases your faith. At that particular moment, the adversary sees an opportunity to creep in and chip away at the foundation of your faith, causing it to weaken in specific areas such as TRUST.

Slowly, trust begins to deteriorate because we have shifted our focus to something, not Jesus Christ. Then, CONFIDENCE decreases in the heart as we envision ourselves unworthy of God's full attention. Some

Christians' anger or disappointments cause them to be defiant, and they use it as an avenue to reject their faith. Such as abandoning their abilities as "Children of God," which includes playing hooky and not attending regular Church service. In essence, the person whom we hurt the most is ourselves. We will never understand why we experience such complex trials. However, the Word of God instructs us to walk upright in every area of our lives.

Even when the confidence level vanishes in thin air, we must find a way to worship or mention the Name of Jesus Christ amid adversities. Listen, churching Sunday to Sunday alone will not build a stronger foundation. We secure our foundation through "obedience and the Love of God."

It is excruciating growing in the knowledge of Christ, and it strengthens relationships with Him. Because experience is evidence of growth, the Holy Ghost is the great Schoolmaster who instructs on remaining connected to the branch. Without the branch, the vine cannot survive alone.

Our faith is the substance of things hoped for and the evidence of things not seen as we trust and place confidence in Jesus Christ, our faith increases. Although we do not see a resolution, by "faith," we believe in the evidence of the supernatural. The promises of God will come to pass, and He will never fail His sheep. Yes, we struggle with faith and are sometimes doubtful or seem doubleminded. Nevertheless, Jesus Christ firmly accepts repentance! So, get into the habit of practicing and learning "how to repent."

Moreover, our hearts are hardened by tough trials and promote stubbornness. But the Word of God, embedded in our hearts, is comparable to a burning fire shut up in our bones. Even as we experience unfavorable events, we know from past experiences that Jesus Christ can bring us through. He has delivered us on the fragmented pieces of our faith and showered us with his love. As a result, the testimonies of his promises are like fire shut up in our bones. When we are weary with forbearing, we can in no way remain quiet.

On the contrary, we share with others how we grew in wisdom. There are different shades of green before a tree reaches maturity. When planted, a seed slowly sprouts and does not remain as a sprout.

It continues to grow until it reaches full maturity, and the flowers or fruit blossom on the tips of its vine. A dark green tree is full of life, and its color remains vivid, attracting lost souls seeking shade, peace, and coolness from the heat.

Those tried by the fire will not smell like they have been in the furnace. They will not smell like fire. The aroma of Victory is the sweet fragrance of God's anointing. So, their knowledge resembles pressed olives pouring savory essences of "wisdom." Providing shade for wandering souls is providing a place where they could rest. Jesus Christ offers opportunities to share testimonies to help another increase in faith and assurance or a sense of coolness to endure fiery trials. Conversating with one another warms the heart, and it bursts with excitement. Sitting to share words of encouragement in similar trials pushes the other to continue toward total devotion to Jesus Christ. After hearing and receiving the Gospel of Truth, the heart burns within us, igniting joy and enlightenment to Scripture. So often, when we hear a sermon, look around, and see some of our brothers or sisters giving God praise and honor, it is plausible that they have received what God had for them.

Teach others how to trust in the promises of God and tell the story of how you made it through to apprehend victory. You will be amazed. Somebody may look back and thank you for allowing the Holy Ghost to use you as the messenger. We are never sure of a kind word's impact when spoken into another's life. Scripture brings and gives new life to the destitute. It is the foundation of our faith to live according to the richness of grace and mercy. So it is through Jesus Christ that we are refined and purified from the wondrous acts of deception. So, we find comfort in the life and characteristics of Jesus Christ.

Apostle Luke wrote did not our heart burn within us, while he (Jesus) talked with us by the way, and while he opened to us the scriptures. The Word of God should warm our hearts with joy and gladness. His Word is a lamp to our feet and a light to our path to lead us out of darkness. And beginning at Moses and all the prophets, he expounded unto them in all the scriptures the things concerning himself.

Searched For Emeralds

1 Chronicles 28:9; Psalm 44:21; Jeremiah 17:10; Jeremiah 23:24; Amos 9:3; Zep 1:12; Romans 8:27; Psalm 139; Psalm 77; Luke 15:24,32; Psalm 89:20; Ezekiel 22:30; Romans 7:10; Philippians 3:9; 2 Peter 3:14; Job 8:16; 1 Corinthians 3; Genesis 28; Genesis 31; Exodus 25; Job 28; Exodus 28; Proverbs 27; Exodus 31; Job 4:19; Job 10:9; Job 13:12; Job 33:6; Job 38:14; Psalm 40:2; Isaiah 29:16; Isaiah 45:9; Isaiah 64:8; Jeremiah 18:6; Daniel 2:33,34,42; Isaiah 1:18; Nehemiah 9; Job 10; Ephesians 3; Psalm 40; Proverbs 4; Isaiah 64; John 8; John 9

Jesus Christ Searches The Heart
"He Knows You"

When looking to find someone, you diligently search for them until they are found. It does not matter how long or where you look. Think about it for a minute: if we spend so much time searching for a soul, why wouldn't Jesus Christ do the same? Jesus is neglected by his people every day, yet he loves us without reservation. He doesn't ask for much in return but for us to serve and walk upright before him. Unfortunately, some believe it is too hard because it means giving up what they want or enjoy doing. The misunderstanding is that they don't comprehend what "giving up" entails. The Lord is not asking us to give-up an entire life for him. And, if he did, it would be justifiable because none of us would exist without him.

On the contrary, he wants us to trade the bad for good habits. Then, start building in a different direction. Why is it necessary for physicians to instruct on eating healthier and we listen? Anything dealing with living holy, introducing souls to Jesus Christ to accept Salvation, is unacceptable. The world quickly crucifies the Saint's faith, upholds hypocrisy, and lives corrupt lifestyles under pretenses.

Still, Jesus Christ, in all "LOVE," offers himself to be Our God and wants us to be His people. So, he searches for 'EMERALDS,' hidden deep in the fiery pits of situations and circumstances. He looks for the castaways, has-nots, broken-hearted, disappointed, and the list is endless. They are determined to receive something new and miraculous when he finds them.

Their hearts are ready to attain Jesus Christ's identity, values, and gifts. It becomes a new journey to rebuild a trusted foundation, which requires hard work, persistence, and obedience. Nothing else matters because the lost Emerald recognizes where the help and love originated. Personal attractions are linked to the ability to understand the love of God in fullness without the merit of pressure.

He searches for Emeralds! He searches and has a deeper understanding of their emotions. The Gospel of Truth leads hearts into total devotion and sincerity. Most likely giving him the glory for acknowledging their imperfections. As such, Emeralds seek ways to get acquainted with the scriptures and apply them to a renewed life.

Jesus Christ searches and know our heart. He tries us and knows our thoughts. He knows your works and criticizes your faith in Him. Often, hearts doubt the authority of The LORD and believe when He has worked out a situation or granted blessings, small or great. Still, some appear ungrateful and are doubleminded in their walk.

Jesus Christ knows the hearts of those who love him despite their adverse failures and temptations. Practice makes perfect! Do not look at the number of times you fall. Instead, look at the number of times you kept going. Over time, you learned to stand and grow tall—like a tree stretching its branches to reach the heights of prosperity. The Spiritual Development in your faith learned to draw strength from a source that provided Supernatural nutrients.

As we mature in holiness, habits are broken, and willpower is defined by the level of trust and confidence placed in Jesus Christ. How can you grow in the Spirit of Righteousness if you never put forth the effort to live according to biblical principles? Holiness, without no man, will see God. So, He gives us sound doctrine to follow and apply to every area of our lives. These actions contribute to the growth pattern and manifestation of the Holy Ghost.

David instructed his son Solomon to know the God of his father and serve him with a perfect heart and with a willing mind, for the LORD searches all hearts. As Children of God, we must learn who is The Father, Son, and Holy Ghost and know their purpose in our lives. After comprehending such things, the heart will perfectly serve Jesus Christ with a willing mind. For instance, as a couple falls in love, they personalize the relationship by learning their partner's likes or dislikes. Avoid behaviors or habits that would upset one another. The main goal is to avoid friction. As a result, the relationship grows because they took the time to learn about the person. Why not use the analogy and love Jesus Christ in the same manner?

The difference between human nature and serving Jesus Christ is that we must abide in His presence, Spirit, and Truth. And The Love of God does not equate to heartbreak. Jesus Christ knows "True Love" and can love you without measure. He personalizes his relationship as each person seeks to understand Him, Reverence, and Accept his authority as King.

Considerably, a perfect heart is where we allow change to occur, and the Holy Ghost serves as our schoolmaster. Emeralds are retrieved from impurities, washed, and treated before the change occurs. Regardless of the moment of truth, get ready, stand up, and accept who you are in the love of Jesus Christ. Call to remembrance your song in the darkest times? You communed within your heart, and your spirit made a diligent search. Jesus Christ searches for Emeralds, and he digs deep to find them.

Stones of Such and Such

Sapphires, gems, and precious stones of such and such, how often do we falter? How often does our heart shatter? There are cracks and flaws on the surface, but deep within, the Holy Ghost fills the cracks with unmeasured oils that are pure and free of impurities.

Diamonds, topaz, onyx stones, and such and such things of the sort. How often do we stumble at the promise outlined in our path? Slipping glasses, impatiently smooth with shimmering attractions, glance at the imperfections, laughing at the flaws. They use our weaknesses for added prosperities, wicked deeds, and childish scenes. Only the LORD Jesus can erase these very things.

What about the beryl stones, emeralds, pearls, and such things that are forgotten and not seen? Pushed aside having no value, God knows how to elevate you. Your thoughts are broad, and your vision is narrowed by the selfish acts of those surrounding you. No, they will not understand your true identity; many can care less about what you feel deep within.

Fire, fire, someone's pants are on fire, for they lie without a cause and tremble at the shame braided by their follies.

The fire ignited by the Holy Ghost burns the things that cause the unfeigned cracks and flaws to blemish precious stones, gems, golden nuggets, and things of such and such had little to tell or sell. The Word of God is a gem, and the Creator, Jesus Christ, is the gemologist. He finds rugged gems hidden and scattered on the Earth. They are gathered from the north, south, east, and west—various individualized gems, from the smallest to the biggest. Somehow, Jesus Christ tailors them to perfection. He washes them in his precious blood, removing the stains of earthly filth, impurities, and pollution. Gently, he smooths all the rugged edges and polishes each gem until it gleams.

Impurities are removed, flaws are diminished, and things are moving like such and such. But who is paying attention to the newness of those precious gems polished and branded new? How long did it take to resemble the gem on the top shelf, placed on the edge, for all to see? How long did it take the gemologist, Jesus Christ, to smooth the rough edges of every gem? They are set in place, whereas none could buy, not even for a cent or two?

Those precious gems belong only to The Father, Son, and Holy Ghost. They are priceless, and their beauty resembles the glory and honor of its Creator. What about all those rubies, pearls, sapphires, diamonds, onyx, and such and such stones of all kinds? The Church will consistently underestimate the value of God's precious gems—as they cannot measure the anointing oil used to erase the defects.

You are a precious gem-shaped and refined by the hand of Jesus Christ. Let the Glory of God shine upon the countenance of your face. Let nothing diminish your shine because you were placed on the top shelf, close to the edge, dangling in plain sight for all to see. Your beauty and self-worth are priceless, a well-crafted Jewel, the only one of its kind.

Jesus Found His Precious Stone

Most of us once believed to have known more than our parents, and whether we were rich or poor did not matter. Many have rebelled because they felt they were much better living on the other side of the door. They believe in enjoying the finest, feasting on its corruption, indulging in lustful desires, and ignoring the warning signs of destruction. In other words, "They are doing them and living it up on their terms. At least, it is what they believe in their hearts. But spiritually, their hearts have died and traveled far into the arms of oppression. They regress into old habits and adhere to wicked, sightless busybodies with unwise counsel.

Our sinful nature causes us to trespass against the Commandments of God. These actions temporarily sever the connection with Jesus Christ because the heart is not engaging in an intimate moment of worship or praise. The dialog is absent, and the spiritual nature of the inner man thirsts for the Living Water. When the branch is disconnected from the vine, it starts to wither and die slowly. Thus, the vessel separated itself from its Creator to partake in sin.

As days progress, they recognize the damage caused. They have torn down the foundation built-up in Jesus Christ with their hands. The pain resulted from the decision made as they wandered as a stranger wearing filthy garments. They are journeying on a path leading nowhere as a lost sheep in a foreign land.

The "STRUGGLE IS REAL" is far from easy to maintain holiness within the Body of Christ. There are so many temptations that are dancing before the eyes. We are trained to resist the devil, and he will flee. Occasionally, some get beside themselves to think they could walk the walk alone and without the support of others. The adversary seizes the opportunity to sift the vessel as wheat. Hence, fiery trials and tribulations are blazing because the "Saint" hardened their hearts and allowed the adversary access to vulnerable areas of their life.

So then, you remember the stance when you walked upright before Jesus Christ. He granted you the opportunity to return and welcomes you without shame. The ramifications are significant, but a heart full of sincerity and repentance is divine. Because when you realize the flaws and personal mistakes, return to the Creator of All Things. Spiritually, the heart is lost! It desires to accommodate its corruptible human natures—having such behavior introduces the wildcard of war between the flesh and Spirit.

Acknowledging faults is to receive the rod of correction for the error of your ways. Jesus finds his precious stones, gently retrieves them, and washes them in His Blood. Heaven rejoices over one sinner who repents more than ninety-and-nine just persons who need no repentance. They did not leave their first love and are justified by righteousness. Unfortunately, a few are not as strong and backslide into old habits because their branches are not as powerful to remain connected to the vine.

A green branch remains green before the sun because it can withstand the intensifying heat. It is deeply rooted and has garnished the productive nutrients to shoot forth in the garden of its work. Jesus finds his precious stones, picks them up, washes them clean, and fashions them into formation. Rugged trails and strong winds will toss your hearts to and from. Emerald, you must adhere to great expectations of holiness. Allow the LORD to create a unique texture design tailored for you. Be transparent in your heart and understand that you are one of a kind. Thou you appear easily broken, Jesus Christ found his precious stone. He will strengthen the fragmented pieces and smooth the rough edges of humility and shame. It does not matter how many times you fall. It matters how many times you get up and keep moving.

When we see others oppressed and vexed in Spirit, we must stand in the gap for their deliverance. Jesus Christ knows the heart of all His people and who would come together as a hedge among us. Stand in the gap and plead before the LORD for those who have gone astray. Pray, make supplication, and petition The LORD to reconcile the broken-hearted. Sin, taking occasion by the commandment, deceives the very elect and kills spiritually. The strong are encouraged to unite, stand, and help fight for continued growth within the Body of Christ. Delight yourself in the Law of God after the inward man, the Holy Ghost, and obey the Gospel of Truth. So, with the mind serve the law of God in newness of Spirit, and not in the oldness of the letter.

Jesus found His precious stone! He dug deep amongst the thorns and briers to retrieve all that belonged to him. Be found in him, not having your righteousness, which is of the law, but that which is through the faith of Christ, the righteousness of God by faith. In pureness of mind, body, and soul, remember to be mindful of the Word of God and do what is commanded of us all. Continue to grow in the grace and knowledge of Our Lord and Savior Jesus Christ.

Extracted Stones

Gems are extracted and cleansed from all debris. When objects are found, we kick around the rubble, pick it up, look over it, and then keep or drop it. If it's found to be of value, the object is saved. Later, it is washed and scrubbed the crevices until its detail is illuminating.

We are bodies of clay broken before the LORD, lost and found. The Love of Jesus Christ extracted us from the brutal reins of life's errant behaviors. From the womb, some of us were shaped by the selfish acts of our parent's iniquities. Still, God found and extracted us from the debris of issues and uncertainty. Standing naked before the "Throne of Grace," crushed stones without formation, a simple vessel needing constant repairing. We look up to God solemnly and say, "Here I am, LORD!" Nothing special, only a simple soul is dwelling in a house of clay designed by you to withstand the perilous times of grit and grind. So often, God's people are entrapped by personal thoughts and imprisoned by human nature, crushed like a moth.

God's people are precious stones extracted from the Earth, cleansed, and polished to perfection. The Creator of Heaven and Earth uniquely designed each earthen vessel to resist sin's clutches. Though our sins are as scarlet, they will be as white as snow; though red like crimson, they shall be as wool. Jesus Christ can uplift and extract his chosen vessels from the pits of shame and confusion.

Some Christians are stuck between acknowledging their flaws and repentance. Many know their duty is to search for God's hand and inquire about personal iniquities. Every soul knows their sin. Unfortunately, stubbornness has caused hearts to rebel against the Gospel of Truth. Now, they began to question their position and whether they were serving Jesus Christ with the utmost of sheer honesty.

Extracted stones are lifted to be formed and cleansed from the filthiness beneath the Earth's surface. Children of God are predestined to shine through the darkness and seek after all righteousness with a pure heart. The hand of God determines who we are and what we become. His hands have made and fashioned us to the perfection of sanctification and truth according to Scripture. The Great I Am made us the clay and gave us life's favor, and his visitation of the Holy Ghost preserves our Spirit. The life granted to us has a purpose and meaning to spread the Gospel of Truth to others. Although we are no longer full of iniquity and lifted from the wells of oppression,

The Lord created his people with wisdom, power, and anointing. We are fearfully and wonderfully made by the hand of a Mighty King. When extracted, we are brought out of captivity and separated from claws of filthiness. The remnant of our faith increases as we continually confess our sins before the LORD of Salvation.

It is good to acknowledge when you are broken! You do not have to feel or think the reflections of shamefulness attack your dignity. Change is accompanied by pain and emotional scars, which will take months or years to recuperate from the sting. Resilience forces us to push beyond personal restraints and bind the heart to the elements of eagerness. So often, life's troubles hold tight to our purpose, and so much time is spent trying to retrieve what others will not let go of in fear of losing everything. So, it is okay to walk away from the things you believe in loving and never think twice about their value. When we are liberated from what we believe "to love," Jesus Christ blesses us tremendously.

Then, we stop to think about it. "God, what have I done so great to deserve such a BIG BLESSING? Then, spiritually, we understood to let go of all the things we thought were essential and held fast to the hem of His garment. Extraction introduces and unleashes a new wave of strength, courage, and anointing because we are now entering a whirlwind of new things that only the Holy Ghost can teach us to sustain.

Extraction deems to let go of the filthiness surrounding "Spiritual Growth." We are branches striving to remain connected to the "Vine," Jesus Christ. Without Him guiding our footsteps, we will never grow to total dependence upon Him. We are accustomed to holding on to sedition, which pollutes and dishonors the body. When taught to wait patiently for the Lord, we are grateful for the deliverance out of the miry clay. The bounds are released, allowing gifts to develop and vessels to emerge as shining "Emeralds."

In the greatness of detail, the fruit of the Spirit is evident in speech and lifestyles. The transformation is evident amongst the unsaved souls.

Jesus Christ is "Our LORD, Father, and the Potter." Extraction is for a set time and purpose, far beyond the imagination or understanding of the fleshly hearts. Extracted stones acquire the mind of God and carry the Word as it is a lamp to our feet and the light to our path. The anointing of the Holy Ghost empowers it to burn with fresh oil while preserving and strengthening with might by his Spirit in the inner man.

Life kicks us around to see if we can absorb its failures. God's people are not built for failure or to resemble dull stones. Jesus Christ has perfect knowledge of every stone regardless of its flaws. He has equipped us to soar far above doubt and fears to build intimacy in praise and worship. The Children of God are elevated in courage and seek complete dependence upon the power of his grace.

We were once cast down, troubled, and oppressed by the filthiness of sin. Now, we are "Extracted Stones," are cleansed and made righteous as a shining light that shines more and more unto the perfect day. We are lights in the world, having the light of life, and we must shine in pureness. Therefore, let us stand tall and uphold one another with love in the Spirit of Truth. There is no respect of person when it comes to serving Jesus Christ.

The Mixed Stones Who Impacted The Emeralds

One significant person has strongly impacted our lives, whether positive or negative. No one can receive credit for your growth in holiness but God. Many have played a part in guiding you in the right direction; still, the anointing of Jesus Christ proceeds the good deeds of those involved. We are vessels of instruments designed to be used according to the divine purpose, which includes building and encouraging the hearts of others to push forward in their ministries. Jesus Christ rewards his people according to their labor in the vineyard. It is never easy striving for "Spiritual Success" when so many looming obstacles and snares are set in motion to destroy your every move.

So, we take a look at the many stones impacting our journey. Stones vary in size, shape, and substance. Trying to figure out a person takes much energy and patience to decipher their true intentions. Possibly, we hope their intentions are good and profitable for building up the Kingdom of God. Souls are hurting and disfigured by the elements of trial and error.

If every soul would grasp the concept of their self-worth, their courage, and faith could move mountains far beyond their boundaries. We are hampered by the struggles attached like heavyweights around the ankles. Our just due is payable by the majestic powers of Jesus Christ. Regardless of the situation or circumstance, remain attentive to His Will. Our attentiveness includes more than attending Church. It is putting forth the works wrought deep within the heart and soul.

For we are labourers together with God: ye are God's husbandry, ye are God's building.

Mixed stones that impacted the lives of "Emeralds" encouraged them to shine. You are God's field of growing souls needing pruning, planting, and watering. Spiritual growth cannot be credited to the hand of man but to God's hand. Humanity is suitable for tilling the ground to plant and grow food. They are not capable of growing the Supernatural gifts of the Holy Ghost. True Believers will strengthen others and build according to God's grace, which is given to us as wise masterbuilders.

Jesus Christ has laid the foundation, designed the path to follow, and set rules to encourage growth in Spirit and Truth. Our growth is defined by how we build upon the foundation of Jesus Christ. His blood polishes away the stain of sin, helping us to resemble Him day-by-day, struggle-after-struggle, and persistence followed by willpower. Learning to surrender all things and casting aside every weight that burdens the heart lightens the load on the journey. We know to delight ourselves in the Words Spoken and the Scriptural Teachings of Holiness.

Let us take heed of how we build upon the Rock of Salvation. First, build a foundation that will illuminate a glow on the countenance of your face. Glow as though you have been in the presence of God, seeking to know more about His statutes and decrees. He is the Creator of all things and Lover to every soul. Yet, many refuse to adhere to the righteousness of power, glory, and honor.

Mixed stones that impact the life of an Emerald could uplift but could not form its shape or fashion its size. The origin of its mineral is defined by the purity of its substance in Jesus Christ. Mixed stones are precious and accent the Body of Christ. We must sharpen the hearts and minds of one another. There is strength in numbers; together, the Saints of God can build monumental goals and soar like eagles if on one accord.

Stones of Encouragement

Stones of encouragement are familiar with remaining in the presence of God and trusting in his arm to deliver and set free. As such, there are certain places where we can sit and find comfort from fiery trials. We build pillows to support our thinking and ease the speed of confusion overwhelming the mind within that place. For a moment, we lay down in that place to sleep because of the peace found. Simplicity ignites a chain reaction associated with clarity because we are not overthinking the issue. Stones of Encouragement are *onyx stones* pillars of strength that accentuate your growth in Jesus Christ.

Stones of Wisdom

Desperation causes hearts to faint and struggle with secular values, which weakens our foundation in Jesus Christ. Nonetheless, sapphire stones full of wisdom are waiting to uplift your soul. They provide wise counsel and are gathered to feast upon the foundation of righteousness. They sincerely give the Word of God, which soothes every corner of the mind. They are filled with the wisdom of God to help others push through the barriers aligned to defeat the struggling Saint. We have all doubted our inability to fulfill what was predestined. So, we look for ways to avoid going in the direction which promotes growth. Doubt causes many hearts to follow deception and destruction.

Onyx stones and stones help to set in place the covenant in the breastplate of righteousness. Many mixed stones are associated with serving God in the fullness of their capacity. Maximizing their love of Jesus to help others build a special relationship upon the "Rock of Salvation."

Engravers

Engravers impact the life of "Emeralds" because of the golden nuggets of epistles. Their testimonies are engraved as signatures upon the tables of the heart. They share the victories Jesus Christ won and how he defeated the enemy for their sake. As we research the scriptures, these stories are etched in our minds, digging for the ouches of gold between the pages from Genesis to Revelations. Stories are engraved in our ancestry's history and depict the genealogy of all who have walked before us. The elders quietly sit, waiting for the opportunity to disburse the "Greatness of Jesus Christ" to every ear, willing to hear the memorials of hope, courage, strength, and power.

Stones of Calmness

Sardius or red rubies are stones of calmness and are constantly on fire for the LORD. They are a team designed to ignite the fire when you feel burned out and exhausted. Leaders of worship and praise serve as the gateway to rejuvenating and refreshing the soul. Learn to adhere to the simplicities of glory. Stop for a minute and revere the Name of Jesus Christ. Do not ask for anything or make your petitions known. Instead, in his presence, offer sincere praises and acknowledge Jesus Christ for the good works wrought in your life.

Building Stones

Topaz stones are illuminating and wise in building walled foundations that keep you on the path of righteousness. Having a team of mixed stones supports and upholds your faith and increases your understanding to remain in the right direction. Iron sharpens iron, so a man sharpens the countenance of his friend. Friends want to push one another to soar like eagles in the face of adversity and disdain. We are programmed to seek what is proper and profitable to the soul. We are commanded to multiply and be fruitful throughout the Earth.

Carbuncle stones are gatekeepers standing in the gap for souls struggling along their journey. They don't mind securing your faith in Jesus Christ. Carbuncle stones are reminders and reiterate God's oracles like a pre-recorded tune kneeling at the throne of grace for the people of God. Without delay, their hearts are programmed to do what is according to the Word of God, which is to strengthen the feeble knees of those who do not know how to pray and seek the help of God for themselves.

Cutting Stones

Cutting stones are those who support your enthusiastic demeanor to pursue your call to ministry work. Without reservation, they are established to oversee your continued growth and provide correction along the way. Sometimes, the correction hurts deeply for perfecting change in the Body of Christ. You will undoubtedly remember their cutting-edge guidance in all manner of quality. Regardless of your stance, they ensure you soar high like an eagle and not faint in well-doing.

A mixture of stones has impacted the life of an "EMERALD." The purpose of their presence is to support growth in vulnerable areas of our lives. Trying to soar on the wings of holiness when weighed down by the pressing issues of distraction and deceit is not easy. It is paramount to be obedient to what is true and righteous according to the principles of God. An "EMERALD" on the top shelf could topple and fall backward into many pieces. But, it must understand that its Creator is the Greatest Gemologist, and He has the power to fix all things.

Swinging From the Edge

Hey, Emerald! Immaculate hues of soft greens and a pinch of blue. Perfection found you a place. Sit here, swing your feet from the edge, and glorify the Gemologist, Creator, and Greatest of All. Look over the mountains at the scenery. It mirrors God's work, and you can see it reflecting from the peak of ocean waves. Admiration fills the heart with peace as it searches for the right words. Day-by-day, not knowing how you came to sit at the edge to see the display of God's beauty and Glory. The world will never know the pain felt from the wounds inflicted by the struggles of hardship and grief. Yet, here you are, sitting for the world to see. You are swinging your feet from the edge—on display in your spotlight. From every angle, your countenance glows with the glistening brightness of purity.

Were you waiting for the opportunity to wave? Of course, many will think you are waving at them and possibly turn their nose up to disagree. But who cares? Never mind the ignorance of their hearts filled with envy. Around their necks, it's fastened like a charm, disarmed by repentance, and later warms their heart.

Only The Holy Ghost understands the wave, offering a simple gesture with the hand. So sit back and relax, rest your thoughts on the victories won from around the world. From one city to another, God held you with high esteem and garnished you with the anointing poured from the palm of his hand.

Glow like the Emerald stone you are, so beautiful and shiny. No one can take your place. The formation is chiseled to perfection, for the course was rough, and fiery trials sharpened your strength. Enjoy the breeze from the nostrils of The King. Sit there in His presence and listen for the stillness of His voice. Wise instruction paved the way for you to attain warring instruments to tear down barriers of disappointment.

A tear fills the corner of the eye, or maybe it's the raindrop from the sky. Sometimes, it feels a tad bit lonely, free from the phony attributes of people who never want to fly high like eagles. So, here you are, sitting on the edge with your feet dangling far above the clouds of disdain. Jesus has broken the chains of settled dreams tucked away in a box like an old sock waiting. The ticking of the clock possibly awakened their hearts to stand tall on the rock.

The Rock of Salvation built the foundation for you to sit high and almost touch the sky. Above the world, they see you sitting on the edge of victory, swinging your feet, and resting from defeat. They thought you lost, never to conquer the wits and fits of life-entangled bows. A one-track mind is how insecurity thinks! They whoa others with fables and myths and never get the jest of realities, checks and balances. So many continue to trip and fumble. They were tumbling over their untied shoes, something so simple—still, they never had a clue. Possibly, it is easier to tremble at fear.

Who will listen and hear the testimonies? None are phony. It is about the greatness which is achieved by the straightness of the walk. Memories of God's Greatness are best perceived from up high, on the edge of victory. You must strive for perfection, grab hold of courage, pull up on wisdom, and follow the paths filled with obedience. There is a spot on the edge of victory for you to sit and dangle your feet far above defeat. They will turn their nose to ignorance from around the world because they lack the beauty of knowledge and the abundance of love.

You can see far beyond the mountains, like an eagle soaring in the sky. Fly in the beauty of holiness! In the presence of Jesus Christ, the air from his nostrils gives the smooth sailings of comfort and peace. Come on up, Beautiful, and rest your feet. Sit here, swing from the edge let your feet dangle against the rays of defeat. Feel the warmth of security and peace. The Sovereignty of The LORD perfects the countenance of the shine from every angle, both far and near. Come, sit here, and wait for the opportunity to wave—a simple hand gesture to share a wave offering, thanking Jesus Christ for the battles he's conquering.

The Measure of Faith

Hebrews 12; 1 Peter; Romans 12; Proverbs 8; Job 12; 2 Samuel 22; Psalm 34; Psalm 37; Matthew 19; Isaiah 10; Ecclesiastes 1; Romans 8; Luke 24; Joshua 23; 1 Peter; 2 Corinthians; Matthew 5; Proverbs 4; 1 Corinthians 10:3; Hebrews 5:12-14; 1 Corinthians 3:2; 1 Peter 2:2; 1 Peter 5:7; 2 Chronicles 19:7; Romans 2:11; Ephesians 6:9; Colossians 3:25; Deuteronomy 32:10; Psalm 17:8; Proverbs 7:2; Lamentations 2:18; Zechariah 2:8; John 7:38; Galatians Chapter 5; Psalm 32, Psalm 49, Psalm 88, 1 Samuel 2, Psalm 18; Psalm 72; Proverbs 11; Song of Solomon 6; Philippians 4:10; John 15; Ezekiel 16;

Sometimes, Situations Are Not For Us to Understand

The trial of your faith

As Jesus prunes, he teaches us to lay aside every weight, and the sin that does so easily beset us and allows us to run with patience the race that is set before us,

He doesn't prune to tear down but to build up and teach how to stand. Why? Because everything and every experience is a testament to another Child of God.

He prunes to build strength and courage.

He prunes to take away the reproach disguised by shame or embarrassment.

When Jesus removes the weights, eyes will see the transformation, and ears will hear the Glorification given to Jesus Christ.

It will be a song with a tune no one can sing but you. So, write it down, sing it loud and clear for every ear to hear, and fear the God of Peace!

Jesus! You reign Supreme.

Jesus! There is nothing you cannot defeat.

Jesus! Your love makes me complete, and this is because you are my everything.

You are the very air I breathe.

My Master, Lord, and Savior.

Hide me from the pain, shield me from the shame

Only Jesus has the power to remove mountains

Take away the disparity and give me clarity.

You are the mind Regulator and Creator of Heaven and Earth.

Make and mold this empty vessel.

Fill it with your Glory so that I can tell the story.

Sometimes, situations are not for us to understand.

Continue to Trust God and Glorify His Name.

Faith Tested

We greatly rejoice when there is peace and the heart is at ease. There's little money in the pocket, bills are paid, children are happy, and the family is in perfect health. The heart's present state is settled in the grace of sufficiency as it silently rejoices for the manifold blessings received.

Sometimes, things can get a bit overwhelming, and we know to pray. But get distracted by mounting problems that weigh heavily and challenge our faith. How we deal with adversities is defined by our judgments and self-control. So, naturally, we struggle with feeling tested by life challenges, and quite often, we question the reasoning for conflicts.

We will never understand the reason, but we would love to learn to go through it without complaining or murmuring. Afflictions are caused by several things, which does not necessarily mean you did any wrong. Every devoted Christian will experience some challenging situation. In advance, there is no concrete plan to help avoid the problem. However, we could practice the correct principles to help minimize damaged emotions.

Knowing how to deal with diverse temptations is not a talent. We must use common sense, trust, confidence, and patience to win. True Believers find comfort in worshipping The LORD and do not focus on the situation. Such action profoundly depends on the personal relationship with Christ. Instead of worrying about going through, they acknowledged Jesus Christ as the "Problem Solver."

Calamities should not destroy your faith. Dissect the problem by applying hourly praise sessions. Do not pray. Rest in offering praise and gratitude to Jesus Christ. It will refocus your mind and give you hope and strength. Make an effort to personalize the experience by creating positive attributes to shine. Not knowing how to go through diverse trails could create a whirlwind of uncontrollable emotions that can topple your faith. So, try making the necessary adjustments to patiently wait on Jesus Christ to project change.

Every day, our faith is tested by life's challenges. Learning to trust the hand of God amid troubling times helps to foster Spiritual Maturity in the Gospel of Truth. Conquering undesirable conflicts will transition to testimonies used as "Story Tellers" to build and edify the hearts and minds of other Christians. Compassionate feelings could encourage others as they face similar challenges. As such, it allows us to explain best how they can conquer negativity by trusting in the divine power of the Holy Ghost.

Emeralds Remain Stable in Jesus Christ

As Saints grow old and progress far into their golden years, many reflect on the LORD. He had given them peace from all their troubles. Current events do not strike their souls because they learned the power of God's promises. He sustained their comings and goings, never left, and continued to bless them far beyond measure.

They tell stories through decades of hymns, serenading ears with humming, soft claps, and slowly rocking back and forth. Then, with their eyes closed, they gently part their lips to say, "The LORD has been good to me, fought many battles, and still is doing great things." So, they leave an inheritance of testimonies from generations declaring how great God is. There is no need to be grammatically correct because the Saints of old did not have much education. Yet, they were familiar with the Power of God's anointing and Saving Grace.

They represent "Emeralds," stable, mature, hard, and strong. They can resist various types of losses and imperfections and recover. The understanding of the journey is to keep moving and pushing your way through the magnitude of harsh circumstances and endure hardness as a good soldier. Moreover, learn to resist the deceitfulness of others by not allowing them to dictate your identity. Although the imperfections are visible to the world, an "EMERALD" remains stable in its place, resisting the oppressions brought on by oppressors. When we do not give another human the authority to rule over our future, we can grasp the importance of seeking The LORD outside the perimeters marked for failures.

Grandparents, Church Mothers, Deacons, and Bishops remind the younger generation to remain steadfast. Lean on Jesus and never let go of his hand. These wise words help create a path for the heart to uphold what it believes to be accurate and profound in every good measure of faith. Adhering to wise counsel makes the perfect wave for surfing into the goodness of courage in the face of adversity. Scratch-resistant has tough skin. Don't be so easily dismayed or discouraged by the behaviors of someone with nothing to offer. Many will not desire the same growth and remain enslaved to wicked deeds. So, they set up snares or traps to manipulate your efforts and stain the ministry you are called to uphold by serving as stumbling blocks. Let nothing persuade your heart to turn away from serving Jesus Christ.

While building, Jesus is busy constructing a path designed for your growth. Thus, no one else could journey on the path intended for you because it is not for them. Everyone has their calling and should seek the LORD for the direction to travel. Since many do not understand the gesture, he drives away the wicked and envious. It allows you to remain devoted and persistent to the Will of God and possess the Gifts of the Holy Ghost. These promises are to those who desire to know and seek The Lord with a sincere heart. In Jesus, we build the courage to keep everything written in His Word. As we experience diverse tribulations, we are enjoined by the testimonies of Wise Saints and should not turn aside to the left or right. "Mature Christians" are no longer part of the world and are called to adhere to the wise instructions of the LORD. Incline your heart to receive the commandments and train your ear to hear the oracles spoken. Separate from the contagious behaviors of idolatry and cleave unto the Lord God. Remain stable, mature, hard, and strong in the Gospel of Truth. The LORD teaches how to chase a thousand because He fights for his people and has never broken a PROMISE.

The Messengers are Emeralds

The sun rises; its reflection sends illuminating light to erase the residue of darkness. Fretful hearts filled with affliction wakes to a better day of newness. A day no one could predestine, but, created by the hand of God as a reminder to prevail and push against adversity. Yet, so many wrestle with the turmoil of darkness, waiting for Sunshine to break through the curtains of despondency.

The Messenger has arrived, bringing good tidings of "Sunshine," a better ointment of love to erase the stains and pain. Tear-stained eyes appear to claim victory but have forgotten Jesus Christ has dried its stream. They are replaced with rays of Sunshine, introducing happiness as a remedy for grief. Pain withers away as the Gospel of Truth strokes attentive ears and slowly occupies the heart, sitting there for a minute or two. The precept of courage outlines the reigns of the heart, digging to unravel the tormenting powers of failure. For a time, "Sunshine" marinates, tucked in a cold spot; it instills seeds of hope, prosperity, and deliverance. Acceptance allows the warmth of love to soothe the aches and pains. The Messengers are Emeralds, chosen of God, to bring good tidings of "Sunshine," a better ointment of love to erase the stains and pain. Listen, receive, and allow the warm rays to penetrate the coldness of the heart.

Hold fast to wisdom and listen to her instructions. Do not let her go; keep her because she is your life. Wisdom is the principal thing; therefore, get wisdom: with all thy getting gets understanding. The moment of perfection has arrived. Release the anguish, let go of the guilt, surrender to the growing powers of the anointing, and achieve victory. Stains and pain are temporary and cannot permanently remain unless the heart grants a pardon. Hey, Messengers are Emeralds, chosen by God to bring good tidings of "Sunshine," a better ointment of love to erase the stains and pain.

Flawed stones such as yourself are destined for perfection. The Blood of Jesus Christ washes away the impurities of filth, melting through the echelons of misery that have thwarted your journey. Come, lend your ear! Hear the oracles of God and hearken to the voice of the Lord. He sent The Holy Ghost to lead the way for the poor in spirit. Their souls are depraved and search for the everlasting love of God. Shuffle through the congested realms of self-pity and look high towards the sky. A new day breaks forth, and the oppressed is free. They are no longer trodden or laughed to scorn. Shame is held at the fingertip of Jesus. He gently strokes the heart until the agony of pain diminishes. Sometimes, the love of God is misunderstood. The lost cannot grasp that he is WHO HE IS to all who believe in the power of his authority and anointing.

In a click of a moment, the slightest change questions your stance on God. Stand still and see the Salvation of the LORD. Shift to the right and reach for a higher calling in Christ Jesus. The disappointments will continue to remain part of this world. There are many broken vessels, some old and others new. Torn by the effects of misery, not wanting to let go of the pain attached to a thing. Instead, some find it easier to hold grudges for years. They are finding themselves stuck in the gloomy rage of sorrow and iniquities. Messengers are Emeralds, chosen by God to bring good tidings of "Sunshine," a better ointment of love to erase the stains and pain.

Stains are not permanent. If it were not the truth, the Word of God would not have told us so. Jesus promised that if we walk in the light, as he is in the light, we have fellowship with one another, and the blood of Jesus Christ, his Son, cleanseth us from all sin.

There are sunny days sent to bring warm rays of Sunshine to cold hearts. Imperfections are corrected through obedience, which leads to perfection. Stains are not permanent. They appear momentarily, and if given the opportunity, they will leave traumatized emotions to last for a lifetime. Messengers are Emeralds, chosen by God to bring good tidings of "Sunshine," a better ointment of love to erase the stains and pain.

Stains obscure our judgment, interfere with emotions, and make it challenging to move forward in happiness. Yet, Sunshine brings hope for a better tomorrow amid the darkest moments. The power of the Blood of Jesus Christ can mend dishonored vessels. The world loves its own and continues to pound its people through rejection. It is crushing hearts, trying to diminish the strength of their souls.

Kneel at the altar, empty your vessel, and pour out the pain, shame, and misery. The world will never show empathy for the troubles you endured. Instead, listen and receive the good tidings and allow the warm rays to penetrate the coldness of the heart. The Messengers are Emeralds, chosen by God to bring good tidings of "Sunshine," a better ointment of love to erase the stains and pain.

The world has nothing to give but the same succulent iniquities from start to end. Look up to the sky and feel the warm rays from the Sunshine. The Messengers are Emeralds, chosen by God to bring good tidings of "Sunshine," a better ointment of love to erase the stains and pain. Listen, receive, and allow the warm rays to penetrate the coldness of the heart.

Find Your Place

Find your place in the body of Christ. We are all precious and created by the hand of a loving God. We are created in the majestic powers of peace, beauty, and tranquility—Jesus Christ designed us to mirror the essence of glory and honor. Our bodies are destined to shine bright. Like the sparkling rays as they dance in the sun in unison to the tune of the wind. The ocean waves are free to flow from one end of the world to another. At its peak, it is not afraid of the raging storms. It goes with the flow and slowly drifts away deep into the fog of mysterious things. The vaporizing mist mesmerizes the minds of all who wish to embark on the journey of uncertainties.

Find your place and free flow in the presence of the Holy Ghost. Allow it to take you on a journey full of certainties. The chosen path is designed for emeralds and other stones to explore the promises written in the beginning.

Find your place and then focus on what is essential to bridge the gap of confusion that tossed your heart back and forth. Relax! Let your thoughts rest in the mysterious, unknown holies of holies. There, you will find a place not hidden but found to become a treasure to those who desire to hold fast to the powers of mercy and grace.

Find your place amongst the diverse stones unknown to man. They are unearthed, found, and shaped according to the hand of their creator. Some stones feel weary and lost, needing guidance to maneuver the rough terrains of iniquities. Yet, they are stones held close to the heart. The Holy Ghost caresses the hand, smooths the cracks of disappointment, and polishes the surface with love.

All stones are not alike, but all are desperate to be made something out of nothing. So those stones hide because they cannot imagine their beauty within. Thus, they remain in darkness, afraid of the form their life has taken.

Find your place and dig deep. Come up to the surface where the light shines bright for the world to see. Emerge with desperation and show up amongst the polluted elements of failure and shame. Hold fast, stand still, look up, and give a wave, surrendering your heart, body, and soul.

Find your place amongst the body of Christ. Never be afraid of the treacherous hearts of the wicked. Their arrogance would never measure to the wisdom or lightness of a stone like you.

Find your place! You are more than what you could ever imagine. You are a priceless gem, unique, exceptional in every way, and the only one of your kind. Stones of the world are pebbles, fragile, and ground to dust.

Find your place amongst the precious stones designed by Jesus Christ. Perfected and molded in the beauty of holiness and instilled to be steadfast against raging storms. Allow yourself to flow freely from one end of the world to the other. Fret not over the things you cannot change. Allow the rays of deliverance to radiate from the surface of the heart and glorify the God of Abraham, Isaac, and Jacob.

Find your place amongst the precious stones, for you are unique and a stone which the Master of all creations greatly desires. Now, find your place, stand tall, and look above the polluted circumstances of failures. Give your wave offering and shine like a unique gem greatly desired by the Master of all creation.

Special Treatment Reconditions the Heart

After accepting Jesus Christ, it is not profitable to continue fellowship with idolaters. Their hearts are not secure in worshipping Jesus Christ and remain committed to sinful habits. Your heart has returned to your first love, which is Christ. You are no longer bound to the worldly provocations set forth to destroy or inflict grievous punishments. A transformation requires unique treatments to spiritually cleanse the heart, body, and soul as a new creature. Renewing the mind requires total devotion and recognition to attain knowledge. Concentrating on the identity as a Child of God, no longer part of the world, is necessary.

You must release yourself from the provocations linked to lustful habits and cling to holy values. The Holy Ghost distributes the knowledge concerning holiness according to the commandments of Jesus Christ. As True Believers, we must not be ignorant but study the Gospel of Truth for wholeness. Therefore, delight yourself in Jesus Christ and mature in the Rock of your Salvation. He has set a new course requiring self-discipline and forgetting old lifestyles.

Jesus Christ will not have his people without knowledge. Our growth in him requires specialized treatments that purge and sanctify. Hence, creating clean hearts and renewing a righteous spirit sets the foundation for reconciliation. The Lord delivered us from bondage—as the generations before us served under the cloud, which is the protection of Jesus Christ. They passed through the sea, received divine care, guidance, and protection, and turned from serving him. As the cloud remained their protection, they were shielded from fiery trials and redeemed from the enemy's hands.

The Blood of Jesus Christ delivered, and by his grace, we are saved. His blood washes away sinful habits and allows us to rebuild according to wisdom, knowledge, and understanding. Most importantly, accepting Jesus Christ makes us peculiar and unique to him. Under his covenant, we receive favor, baptism of the Holy Ghost, and heavenly gifts. We must serve under the Biblical Laws of righteousness and feast on the manna from on high.

Gems are precious stones that require special treatment to help us shine like a light. The world lives in darkness and does not know Jesus Christ as its Savior. We cannot feast upon the corruptible fruit which entangles our purpose and diminishes our light. Once, we ate the same spiritual meat and drank the same spiritual drink. But, some have fallen and are separated from the Kingdom of God. They no longer desire the bread of heaven, which came to save us. Neither do they thirst for the water that streams from the rock, and this Rock is Christ.

Instead, their hearts desire to remain broken, unstable and lost to generational practices that are unwise and deceitful. Following Jesus Christ is to drink from the stream that flows from the Rock while in the wilderness. He has given divine instruction to the Holy Ghost, who can teach us how to build and believe in Jesus Christ. As the scripture has said, out of our belly shall flow rivers of living water. Believers are to drink from the Rock and be filled. It is a privilege to be saved and eat the spiritual meat containing the Word of God, which is holy and acceptable.

Transitioning from the old into the new is not easy and requires a willingness to walk in agreement with the promises. We have a divine commission that is different from that of the world. Those who are not careful will fall and be overthrown in the wilderness. Our faith must increase in Jesus Christ and not come short of the Glory of God. Profess all true things and turn from wickedness. The "Love of God" has uprooted us from the bonds of iniquity and planted us firmly in his House to glorify and worship his name.

Sprouting Changes

Sprouting is budding, rising above, and reaching the source that causes growth and development in our faith. The Holy Ghost is the source that nourishes our continued growth in the Body of Christ. It communicates and teaches the law of righteousness, builds confidence through the LORD, and helps us obey the truth. Yet, we often forget how to continue moving towards our goals in ministry because we are easily distracted, slow to believe, and without understanding.

Life struggles are channeled as distractions that deplete our desire to pursue greatness. They are constant reminders of past disappointments and failures. Yet, although we stumble, there is a window of opportunity to prevail against life's challenges. The Lord Jesus will give us the strength to battle and perfect our way.

When the journey darkens, we lose sight of essential things that elevate our belief. Trials and tribulations prevent many from moving forward because they focus on things that do not matter. Press through the thickness of the storms and flourish like the grass of the earth. Jesus Christ sustains his people, and the righteous flourish as a branch. The branch can continue growing if it remains connected to the Vine. Jesus Christ sent The Holy Ghost as a Comforter, and his people can find everlasting consolation in Him.

Jesus Christ, the "True Vine," purges every branch so that it may bring forth more fruit. We are the *(branches)*; SPIRITUALLY CONNECTED to Jesus Christ. Hence, to grow and produce fruit. The LORD is our foundation; without him, it will deteriorate and crumble. In all, the fruits of righteousness are evident through the Holy Ghost. It will deliver purity and power if the branch remains rooted in the Vine. Spring forth! Abide in the "Vine," as the branch cannot bear fruit of itself, except it abides in the Vine.

Therefore, do not waste time on things that do not matter. They will continue to stunt growth and development in Jesus Christ. So often, the minor thing we spend so much time thinking about—gives wasted time to a platform. One of the adversary's most potent tactics against vulnerable minds is confusion. When confused, we stare into outer space, pondering on the next move and hoping it will fall into our laps. Sometimes, we cause such deranged thoughts to feel our minds because of spiritual insecurities. Our confidence level in "trusting God" is at an all-time low. Quickly, we give *"I can not, and I am afraid"* more power than it deserves. Change is scary on all levels, but trusting in The Holy Ghost to carry you through fear to grow and build your relationship with Jesus Christ.

Feeling confused and without direction will dismantle our faith because we allow "doubt" to interfere with biblical principles as true believers. Therefore, the blame lies with us, and we have the power to change our stance. Spiritual insecurities are the very things that keep us from pursuing what we need to achieve in ministry. If everything related to spiritual Wellness is not adequately nourished, we feel malnourished in prayer, praise, or worship. Rejoice in the LORD! Do not lack the opportunity to flourish. Let us take pride in the Gospel of Truth and reach toward the Light of Salvation, which has cleansed us from the works of iniquities.

For instance, if our hearts are focused on something that has genuinely caused great disappointment, we lose our hunger for seeking God because we are intensely focused on one life-changing event. As such, everything around us comes to a screeching halt. Not focusing on ministry or spending time with God, be it in prayer, praise, or worship, or reading the word of God, we forget to feed our vessels the talents they need to go deeper in serving Jesus Christ. Sorrowful changes would significantly impact our walk as true believers. The heart loses interest as it branches out to see what it believes is more interesting than the current lifestyle.

Some people believe prayer is boring, and worship has become so overwhelming with overrated lyrics that the ears are no longer attentive to the musical tunes. In addition, some people view prayer as boring because many do not know how to communicate with God through the Holy Ghost.

But, what many people don't understand is that you do not have to be in prolonged prayer with God, but knowing how to communicate openly with him is building a relationship. While building a relationship with God, show total dependence on him. In return, Jesus Christ will work out and fulfill every area of our lives. When we begin to understand this, then we know that there is a sprouting change or a sprouting bud that has taken place in our walk with the Lord.

When we do not see or feel the change, it discourages growth. Hearts will wax cold as many feel they are not growing or drawing closer to the Lord. Get in the habit of practicing and speaking to The LORD. Regardless of the time of day, He is ready to engage in a holy conversation with you. Prayer creates personalized relationships, and the Holy Ghost will start interceding on your behalf. Some things in life are not always "hard pills to swallow."

We make it difficult when it's not complicated. But, we thank God for wisdom, knowledge, and understanding because when we know how to communicate with God, we do better. Many people are receptive to short, two-minute prayers. Thus, a 20-minute prayer is warranted to be too much, which is not long. In my opinion, it is a warmup before the breakthrough. But, so many people are accustomed to shorter prayers.

They have heard generations before prayed for long periods. They have not grasped the purpose of prayer. Some people don't want to be bothered because they believe the old way or traditional practices of the Church are outdated. It is not that the old way of praying is obsolete. Older generations prayed in their heavenly languages, such as (speaking in tongues); or crying before the throne of grace. These ancient customs remain necessary and profitable for the gem willing to continue its growth.

Unfortunately, the new Millennium doesn't understand the concept of prayers. Preferably, five-minute or two-minute prayers are sufficient enough for them. Thus, they believe it to be just enough to speak with God. But understand this one thing: communication is critical. In Jesus Christ, we must learn to communicate with Him through the Holy Ghost daily, reciting and searching biblical scriptures. Anything we want to know about him is in the volume of the book. When you gain wisdom, a sprouting change takes precedence, ruling over the old habits. The heart delights itself in the knowledge of God, and its branches are no longer withering and losing their vividness. Instead, it shows evidence of life growing greener in The Holy Ghost.

So many hearts are anxious for so many other things that a conversation with the Lord is unnecessary until many begin to faint and grow weary and well-doing. People genuinely believe that they can prostitute God. What do I mean by prostitute God? They genuinely believe that they can use God when they want to use God and throw him away. But it's hard to kick up against the prick because Jesus Christ is the blesser, Jesus Christ is the deliverer, and Jesus Christ is the one that makes ways out of no way when you're standing there looking like the adversary has blindsided you. But learning to yield to the gospel of truth inspires sprouting changes. Instead of growing so vastly, try taking the long route and gain strength and courage to tackle elements of disappointments one problem at a time.

Developing and Sprouting in salvation does not happen overnight. It takes much persistence, diligence, willingness, and courage to follow after the things of God. And do what God has called you to do. Stop looking at other people and the techniques used to exalt The LORD. Find your unique style and do not "copy-cat" or mimic the ways of others; it is such a bad habit that it may cause you to err.

Ask the LORD for your unique style. If you must mimic someone with pride, follow after Jesus Christ, a perfect example of Glory and Honor. *"Understand who you are and accept whose you are,"* doing what you have been called to do, focusing on what you need to do. The Holy Ghost will do the rest as you begin to focus on yourself. Stay tuned and connected with the Vine as the branch, nourishing a sprouting change. As we take our time to familiarize our hearts with the precepts of God's word, the Holy Ghost awakens, allowing us to hear and prepare to receive the good tidings for building the foundation from the roots to the outer appearance.

The sprouting or evidence of God's word will live fruitfully and bountifully on the inside, waiting for the opportunity to blossom in the Beauty of Holiness. Spiritual growth reflects on the outskirts of life's challenges. There is no other way to bring about a sprouting change without the evidence of the Holy Ghost, the fruit of the Spirit.

When we plant a seed in a pot of soil or place it in water for a duration, it begins to take root. As a result, we see a sprouting change of greenery that represents life. Living according to God's commandments is never an easy task. We continue to seek good and profitable things for our souls to grow and develop in the commandments surrounding righteousness.

We desire to yield and live righteously for the Kingdom of God. Making the necessary adjustments is according to the promises outlined in the Gospel of Truth. We apply the scriptures as a sap to open wounds for healing and deliverance. Choosing change inspires us to trade in the fragmented pieces of our lives for wholeness in Jesus Christ.

We fell short in serving the Kingdom of God when confronted with disparities. However, the Holy Ghost quickens our faith through songs, messages, prayer, worship, or any avenue God uses to deliver His Word. We must train ourselves to become subject to the life of holiness. The Holy Ghost tailors a life acceptable to the oracles of God, which we have heard and learned from the testimonies of others.

The Holy Ghost tailors a life acceptable to God's oracles if we allow him to lead and follow. It takes a willing heart to depend upon the strength and right hand of Jesus Christ. Depending upon ourselves will cause us to trip over our feet. Search the scriptures for guidance or change our hearts and minds to align with God's commandments. As such, we ask God to give ear to the desires of our hearts and grant strength to remain steadfast. By his right hand, he can save and restore his people from the dreadful afflictions of deception driven by the reproach of the enemy.

The guidance of Jesus Christ is evidence of his defined favor showering upon the vines whose hearts are filled with troubles. His love has delivered us from the land of Egypt, a time of oppression and wickedness. So, let us continue to move and seek after the Kingdom of God in search of a sprouting change that would exalt us in his presence and humble us towards total dependency on the Living King. Jesus encourages his people to multiply as the buds in the field, increasing in greatness and confidence.

Humbled is The Settled State for Perfect Endings

Humble is the settled state after experimenting with trial and error. The faulty starting point that never goes right is the straw that broke the camel's back. An old idiom is simply saying, "you are fed up!" Finish with the disappointing factors that seem right, but is it right according to personal standards?

Well, trial and error teach us how to remain humble. Bursting into moods filled with grumbling and repetitious behavior pushes you closer to the edge of defeat. So, take a few steps back, inhale deeply, and exhale. Stand there, look at the problem, shake your head, and walk away. Keep your posture. Humbleness is a new starting point. Excitement tickles the funny bone, wherever that is, but you find yourself laughing at the mistakes. They are learning factors that push the correct buttons for panic attacks and worrying about things you cannot change. Take it in stride—do not look back at the crooked paths of foolery and deceit.

It's a trick to entangle your mind and fill your heart with disappointment. Laugh, setback, and relax. There is nothing to worry about because worrying brings confusion and self-doubt. What on earth will you do with "self-doubt?" If you do not believe in yourself, no one else will try to trust you.

Whistle and slowly walk away from the arrogance when it refuses to listen to wise counsel. Their hearts yell from deep within their reigns. If you get any closer, you might hear the rapid rhythm dancing to a tune of impending slips and falls. Yep, they have confided with their inner voice and devised a plan called "self-sabotage."

There it is—tumbling walls of disobedience echo from the hostile forces of frustration and anger. Standing in the array of self-pity, you wish to say, "I told you so." Saddened emotions freeze our stance where we cannot move or speak. Instead, the HUMBLENESS of our hearts opens our arms wide to offer comfort to hardened hearts.

Once upon a time, we all traveled the road of doing what we wanted and did it with deaf ears. The voice of reasoning did not have a chance to blow its horn loud and clear. We quickly stopped its opinion before it could resonate from the tunnel of hope. So, we sit on the front porch of our faith, conversing with God about the overflowing spills of mercy and grace. Searching afar for the turning point of the loss to adhere to the whispers of "I messed up and thought it would work my way."

Shame and the bands of trial and error tell stories of unique struggles. HUMBLE beginnings to PERFECT endings are the settled parts of life where we have learned to endure hardships and adapt to changes. Life has a list of lessons to teach, and we offer a cheat sheet for those who desire to learn the easy way and minimize the hardness of the heart. The "Emerald Stones" on the top shelf understand that the struggle is real. Most importantly, the God it serves upholds them with love and care. A stone that remains in its crown is secure in the hand of its Creator. We sit on the top shelf, watching and waiting to encourage the hearts of those willing to listen to wise counsel.

Greener Things are a Mixture of Greens

Mark 8, Matthew 16, Deuteronomy 8; 2 Chronicles 1, John 15, Luke 23:31, Isaiah 58; Galatians 5, Ephesians 5; Psalm 92; Ezekiel 2; 1 Peter 1; Isaiah 51; 2 Kings 7; Jeremiah 14; Psalm 118; Lamentations 4; Genesis 30; 1 John 2; Deuteronomy 6; Hebrew 5; Job 15, Numbers 13, Psalm 92:13; II Cor. 5:7; Hebrews 11:1; I Corinthians 15:1-4; I Corinthians 16:13; Gal. 2:20; Col. 2:6; Deuteronomy 8; 1 Corinthians 14; Deuteronomy 6; Isaiah 41:10; Ecclesiastes 7:10; Proverbs 1:20-22; Psalm 33:20

Green with Envy

Have you ever desired something? Or, wished you could own a small portion of another's goods? We have experienced the taste for another person's things and not know we envied their life. Possibly, you used your peripheral vision to stare at something or someone, pretending to ignore their nice things. It makes you laugh, huh? But is it a part of nature for us to do such a sad deed? If the truth is to be told, I envied everyone who had better than me.

It made no sense for some to struggle harder than others. Deep within the heart, we begin to build up resentment and anger. We desperately sought someone, a situation, or something to blame for the lack. Let us not forget that we blame EVERYTHING on The Lord. We never stopped to evaluate our current position and search for a better plan. Nope, the whining got louder and more annoying as the years passed.

Our hearts were green with envy. We allowed jealousy to take complete control, blurring our vision. So, we could not see which direction to take or the path to travel. Instead of growing into wisdom, knowledge, and understanding, we chose to walk in reality. Awakened by the diversities of life's twisted turns and upsetting changing events, we remain lost to the elements of failure.

Failure becomes a cycle woven deeply into the fabricated lies produced by society. The world has a set of values designed to question your survival skills. You might have felt alone at one point, thrown to the side like a raggedy doll or broken toy. Harsh words, huh? Life throws hard punches. However, we can duck and dodge the punches or take the beat down. I do not know about you—but I'd rather fight back and claim my spot.

Green with envy destroys dreams and causes setbacks. Focus not on what another has because it takes too much time and energy. Being jealous of someone or desiring their things will not improve your position. Think about it for a second. Whatever it is, cast the thought down and focus on you. You can have the finer things in life as well. To achieve greatness, you have to apply yourself. It is best to take a moment and sit down and think about the importance of your salvation. Having the finer things in life is not wrong, but we must not be careless in handling all the gifts entrusted to our care.

For what shall it profit a man if he shall gain the whole world and lose his soul? Remember, Jesus Christ is the "Great Blesser," and prosperity reigns with him. The Earth is the Lord and the fullness thereof and all that dwells in it. We will never own anything if the world has to give it to us. Count up the cost? Would you prefer to have Jesus bless you or the world? Do you believe it is forever after the world has allowed you to build a noticeable reputation, power, prominence, and wealth? Earthly gifts are tangible and temporary. The gifts of Jesus Christ are eternal, and no one has the power to take them from you.

Being green with envy causes you to forfeit your soul. Do not worry about the things of this world. It has nothing to offer! It is full of sinful acts and mischievous deeds. There are consequences for greed, and reproach is not far behind. So, please don't lose your life trying to gain from it. There is much to gain from the Kingdom of God; with him are heavenly gifts that are priceless, and only his people can apprehend them. Embrace yourself and continue to seek what is good and profitable to edify the soul, heart, and mind. Whatever the unsaved have, you can have better. Continue to follow Jesus Christ and live according to biblical principles of righteousness.

A Green Tree Is Better Than A Dry Tree

A green tree is ripe, flourishing, strong, fruitful, and has a chance to produce seeds. It welcomes life to share its fruits with those lacking proper nourishment. It offers strength, shelter for the wandering souls, and fruit for the poor. A green tree will continue to grow tall whether the seasons change and its roots reach deeper to secure its foundation. A strong tree can withstand raging storms and tempest winds. Its branches stretch far and wide toward the sun and are a nesting place for the fowls of the air.

The analogy of a green tree is used to describe the flourishing characteristics of God's people. The healthy vessel has the potential to cement its foundation in Jesus Christ. Our self-worth is determined by the amount of time spent with the planter, allowing him to manifest and bring forth the fruit of the Spirit. Without abiding in the vine, we will be like a dry tree without the proper substance to produce for the Body of Christ.

Jesus is the true vine, and his Father is the husbandman or plowman who tills the soil, preparing it for planting. The LORD breaks up the hardened substances by cleansing us through the word and washing away sins in the Blood of Jesus Christ. Repentance breaks loose the chains of bondage. We are no longer captive enslaved people bound by the oppressor or sin. Once freed, we are given the liberty to choose life and accept Jesus Christ as LORD and Savior. Confession is the first step taken to rebuild on the Rock of Salvation. As we continue to profess our relationship with Jesus Christ, we can surrender and submit to the power of the Holy Ghost.

Afterward, the heart becomes fresh soil, prepared and ready to receive the seed, which are the commandments and promises of the Gospel. A hardened heart is a stiff-necked vessel refusing to repent and rejecting pruning, which encourages growth. Thus, its leaves start fading to brown, soon breaking off from the vine and backsliding to old habits. As a result, its branches wither and break. Every branch abiding in the "True Vine" that produces not the fruit of the Spirit, Jesus Christ takes it away. Otherwise, the branch has the power to stunt the growth, contaminate or corrupt willing vessels.

Every branch the remains in and attached to the vine produces fruit. Jesus Christ continues to purge us by delivering, healing and forgiving us for our transgressions. Accepting the purge determines our ability to grow deeper roots to secure our stance against the adversary. Obeying the commandments of God, as written in the Gospel of Truth, cleanses us through the Word.

Continuously seek a life of holiness; without Jesus Christ, we can do nothing. He is the central location, the foundation on which we build. A green tree's foundation begins with a strong foundation. Properly nourished roots will strengthen to maintain sanctification and glorification. A green tree is justified by the fruit it produces. The fruit of the Spirit is love, joy, peace, longsuffering, gentleness, goodness, faith, meekness, temperance; against such, there is no law. Therefore, the fruit of the Spirit is in all goodness, righteousness, and truth.

Someone who has experienced only hurt or afflicted others will not understand good. So, they reject good and trade it for evil. Jesus wronged, not a soul. He loved, healed, delivered, and performed miracles for all and the Father, who, without respect for persons, judges according to every man's work. Those who chanted crucify him rejected love and traded it for sedition and murder. They were accustomed to receiving the brut of life. When Jesus comes on the scene, sharing the love of God and performing miraculous works that no other could do, humanity rejects good. People are prone to dealing with adversities produced by the afflictions of burdens. Accepting hardship and mistreatment is an everyday norm because generations are taught to concede.

God's people do not concede to the diverse tactics of the enemy. We have to resist the adversary and accept the goodness of Jesus Christ. Stop! Sit down, evaluate your family tree, and search for the "Fruit of the Spirit." Are there green or dry trees? These things are passed down from generation to generation, creating a melting pot of anger, depression, and oppression.

A dry tree is good for nothing. Its roots are decayed because it lacks water for restoration and power. Thus, its roots wither under burdens, and the vessel rejects the ventilation or freshening it needs to grow. The

Holy Ghost exalts the horn like the horn of an unicorn to anoint the vessel with fresh oil. As trees grow, they are exposed to the atmospheric elements of inclement or enjoyable weather. As such, the Children of God are exposed to the atmospheric conditions or elements of danger and chaotic circumstances. However, we could choose to live and allow the Holy Ghost to teach us how to stand firm and entrust our "Spiritual Growth" to the husbandman.

We are the branches abiding in the True Vine, who allowed us to come forth from our mother's womb. Every soul did not birth itself into existence. Jesus Christ oversaw the Father's creations from beginning to end and oversaw the growth of a pregnancy from a seed (embryo) through a full-term birth until you exited the womb and inhaled a breath of fresh air. Thus, you lived! A green tree of righteousness does not have the power to grow independently.

The workers of iniquity continuously fight against the trees of righteousness. Knowing the enemy's attacks will not cease, Jesus Christ sent us a Comforter to shield, help, and teach us how to survive inclement danger. Often, here in Florida, we are prone to hurricanes and tornadoes. The National Hurricane Center continuously provides updates, warnings, watches, and forecasts when a hurricane brews in the Atlantic. It informs on the storm's severity from tropical to significant hurricanes. During the storm's eye or amid the storm, the meteorology team of experts spends hours guiding the people through the storm. Thus, we are warned before destruction hits. In remarkable similarity, the Holy Ghost gives warning before destruction through diverse teaching and preaching of the Gospel of Truth. Children of God can choose to listen, build their faith, or turn a deaf ear.

Growing in Christ is not easy! I will be the first to admit it as a fact. There are briers, thorns, and scorpions growing with us. Please do not be afraid or dismayed by their looks because they are powerless. Scorpions are predators who hide during the day and are active at night. They are a rebellious house that desires to remain in darkness and avoid the light. Indeed, if bitten by a scorpion, its sting can cause great harm. Still, we have the power to resist their fruitless perils and reach for the righteous fruit of Jesus Christ.

A green tree needs sunlight as an energy source to grow tall, more robust, and more fruitful because our light must shine before men. Adhering to discouraging behaviors of others taunting your growth is compared to moths eating away at a garment of righteousness. The stain of sin left untreated on a righteous garment attracts moths. A moth attaches itself and destroys the garment because it refuses to obey the Gospel of Truth. If the roots of a green tree are left untreated, insects will cause it to decay, becoming a dry tree lacking the proper nutrients. Either grow with the help of the Holy Ghost or wither away like a dry tree, which is good for nothing, and cast away.

The grace of God is given to those who serve him, allowing them to shine bright as the sun. The horns of a unicorn reach their greatest height and in their wholesome form. We can receive the fresh anointing in abundance to grow older with wisdom, understanding how to renew our Spirit in Him. Producing good fruit is evident that Christ has revived our Spirit with the richness of his mercy. As a result, we cannot grow in traditional life values because generational sins, superstitions, and old wise tales customize them.

The trees of the LORD are full of sap and stand tall like the cedars of Lebanon planted by Jesus Christ to dwell in the habitation of God and The Holy Ghost. Those he has grown are full of the sap of holiness to flourish in His courts. Diligence adds to their faith, virtue, and knowledge to continue producing the fruit that represents God's honor, power, and glory forever. Fresh oil helps renew our faith, comforts our souls, and represents our identity as green trees of righteousness. Although we are planted in a world of corruption, sin does not entitle us to remain in its contaminated soil. We are replanted in the House of the Lord to take root, secure a solid foundation, grow as tall as the cedars in Lebanon, and flourish in his courts according to his divine power and plan.

Why Sit We Here Until We Die

Why sit here until we die? Every day, we face different situations and seek a resolution. Growing up, we never understood why struggles have become part of life, whether good or bad. Yet, we continue to push beyond what others may seem impossible. It is on the tip of their tongues to ask, but they dare not to inquire because of the dangers involved in conjuring up an endless conversation. In the far thoughts, they are thinking, "why did I ask?" It is funny but true. Some Christians may feel the same and ask themselves, why did I ask Brother or Sister a question? No one is ever ready for the response received, whether good or bad.

While striving to secure Holiness and wearing wisdom as a yoke around the neck, every day, we want to live according to the commandments of God. So, we inquire within ourselves about the ramifications of not staying in the Will of God. Why sit here until we die? We have the power to live and do according to what the Father commands. We are destined to live in the greatness and pureness of His glory and honor. Someway or possibly somehow, we missed the chance to live as we decipher the hidden messages between the pages of the Word of God.

Our lack of thirst causes us to die a spiritual death produced by starvation. Every day, our inner man desires to be fed the promises of God. Yet, we continue to fall out of desperation and stagnation. We are stagnated because we do not understand how to grab hold of The Holy Ghost and not let go until he has taken us higher and deeper in the realm of Holiness, Sanctification, and Purity. Quickly, we are shaken by diverse acts of turmoil which cause us to tremble in the depths of the soul. Others look upon the countenance of our faces and see the turmoil and pain written from one side to the other.

Why sit here until we die? Obedience is better than any sacrifice, and learning to embed these simple words in the heart and mind will push you far beyond what you ever expect yourself to reach. Learning to feast on the Word of God is learning to study and dig for the understanding between parables and verses.

Rugged stones are dug up and washed, and all impurities are removed before the formation begins. Never let past decisions or life circumstances determine your start in acceptance of Jesus Christ. Once you are in…he will do the rest of the work. What is required is "OBEDIENCE" and a will to change everything about the old you. Jesus Christ is ready for all to receive and take Him up on his ability to LOVE despite ALL.

A famine is in the land because many are dying from a lack of knowledge, wisdom, and understanding. The leprous men knew a change had occurred in their lives, which caused a separation from the City and its people. As they looked around, weighing their options, they got up and did something to change their current position. Get up, Look around, acknowledge your current position the shortcomings, and make a move.

Listen, Friend, all Christians struggle with refraining from sin. However, many do fall! Your walk in Jesus Christ is similar to a toddler learning to walk. Each time you fall, you must get up, and keep trying. Never give up because a perfect gemstone has endured the formation into perfection. Thus, you become the "EMERALD STONE ON THE TOP SHELF." Jesus placed you in a position to shine amid raging storms, trials, and tribulations.

Emerald stones are imperfect, unique stones and are identifiable by different hues of green. The analogy of the stone paints a portrait of the growth phases Christians achieve in the Body of Christ. The pressure to live righteously and trying to bridge the gap of uncertainties wearies the soul. Every day, we struggle to build a foundation in Jesus Christ to attach ourselves to Him permanently. We worry about the pressures from others by applying the Word as constant reminders to do good. It is funny, but sometimes the grip of the Holy Ghost is so tight that even when we try to do bad, He keeps us. As a result, the mind allows weird thoughts to attack your sanity. Unknowingly, you are standing strong on the foundation of holiness, serving Jesus Christ to the best of your ability. You have done nothing, but all are accountable to "OBEDIENCE." The Love of God is honest and will never fail.

So, why sit here until we die? Why die in the arms of sin when we know that Jesus Christ is a keeper to all who desire holiness? Yes, it hurts to live holy because you have to deny the fleshy lusts and live up to the standards written by the finger of God. There will be times of loneliness, whereas tears will slowly flow from emptiness. Guilt and shame overcrowd your purpose because of your inability to explain the desire to uphold the commandments of God. The heart searches for seasoned words to build up and not tear down the weakness of others. Sometimes, words spoken will not be received accordingly.

Why sit here until we die? Pursuing holiness or having a thirst for righteousness separates you from others. Holiness involves sanctification, and everyone will not pursue what is good. On the contrary, many will continue to adhere to the cravings of their flesh. They are not ready to walk beside or with you. So, why sit here in this state of mind until you die? Spiritually, you are dead to wicked deeds of sin but alive in Jesus Christ.

At the gate entrance, the heart awakens by the stance of starvation. The famine has caused a drought, the soul thirsts for the living water, and the vessel is empty. Iniquities testify and speak on sin's backsliding natures because many have enabled themselves to be overtaken by lustful desires. Together, we are ashamed and confounded because, as strangers journeying in a foreign land, our eyes failed to focus on the prize, Jesus Christ.

Why sit here and die? Man has not power to save or deliver in times of trouble. Seeking the world's vanities separated many from the love of God. They disgraced themselves when they broke the covenant with The LORD, who kept their feet while they went astray. Why fall into the hands of the enemy? Undoubtedly, the enemy will consume you without mercy and has no power to save you. Why wander into the territorial realms of deceit and anguish? The enemy has to kill the ministries of God and cause a spiritual separation. Why sit here and die?

If you enter into the arenas of sin by obeying the flesh, surely you will die because it is starving and wants its appetite to be satisfied with occasional sins. If you say you will give into fleshly natures, the famine will destroy and eat away at the center of your faith. The foundation in Jesus Christ and your Christian values slowly start to deteriorate. Why sit there and die from poor decisions that would not strengthen your stance? Instead, the famine within your soul wants to be fed corrupt fruit. If you do not do something about the famine, you will die from the side effects and hunger pains. After eating, hunger pains subside, but are you willing to give it and suffer outcast to desolate places with God? There is no good reason to choose famine and leave attributes of holiness on the side. Stepping outside the realms of holiness is detrimental to "Spiritual Maturity." Restoration is hard work to get back into complete devotion to The Lord. It is now a phase of "Total Surrender and Absolute Devotion." A type of commitment that is achieved through "Fasting and Praying." Laying down holiness is not a good idea. Later, you try to regain your place—only to find that the gift has been dismantled.

Why chose to fall unto the host of the Syrians? Will they not crush you and sift the good ornaments of wisdom, knowledge, and understanding far from your reach? Their speech will begin to entice your ears, and confusion changes your thinking. In a split second, your heart questions your purpose. What are you to do or say? A little taste will hurt a great deal. It will hurt your pride, destroy your image, and tarnish your image with God. Yes, we know Jesus Christ forgives and can wash away the sin. But why challenge the powers of the God you serve?

Faith is the substance of things hoped for and the evidence of things not seen. Walk upright in your Faith and Jesus will do the rest. Lack of knowledge and common sense cause many to fall short in perseverance. The four leprous men knew there was a famine and regardless how things looked, they refused to sit there and wait to die from the effects of the famine. They sought for a solution and weighed their options. Christians are outcast separated for the good of the Kingdom of God waiting to be used according to their faith.

Why take a bruising from the enemy by allowing them to extract the Word of God from the heart and leaving you as an empty shell, lost, and confused. Don't sit there and die! Choose life and drink from the living well of water which quenches the thirst for the worldly lusts. As we evaluate our current state of mind, sometimes we laugh because we are saddened by how we allow ourselves to fall short of the Glory of God.

Regardless of how hard we try; it appears our position never changes. When the change is invisible, continue to pursue righteousness. Wait for the change which is not always visible to the naked eye. Why sit in the same position until you completely die? Get up and do something! Change takes place each time a step is made be it backwards or forward. The wrong step could have an impact which can become detrimental to the level of survival.

Every day, the flesh dies to sin so that you can build on the Rock of Salvation. However, sin has the potential to destroy who you are as a "Child of the Living God." Be careful for what you are doing and know who you are while doing whatever it is you do. Christians fail to "keep it real," with other Christians. As a result, the brother or sisterhood crumbles under pressure leaving one to suffer from the adverse effects of spiritual warfare.

Why sit we here until we die? If you fall in the hands of the enemy, he will destroy your identity, purpose, and ministry. So, you have to dig deep and understand the war you are in is "your battle." A battle fought by Jesus Christ, because he has given the Holy Ghost authority to teach his people how to war against the adversary. Yes, we are frighten and frantically run for shelter from the arrows. Our soul become weary at well doing and suffer from the estranged tricks of deception and defeat. We die because fear has traumatized our thinking and crippled our prayer standards. Slowly, we began to drift away from worship and omitting exalting the Name of the Jesus Christ.

It is sad! But, True. Remaining truthful to your shortcomings are an awakening act to perfect what is flawed and no longer distinct. When a flaw is distinct, it simply means you have conquered the habit and the residue associated with shame, pain, and pity are no longer applies to self. It is not distinct if you still can feel the effects of sin in the heart. Where is the deliverance? Receive the deliverance and trust that you are alive in the Gospel of Truth. The Word gives life! Live in the abundance of mercy.

The four leprous men knew they were separated from others because of their condition. Yet, they refused to sit there in one spot and die. Regardless which way they went if they fell in the hands of the enemy; they knew the end would be death. So, the men got up and did something to change their current position.

Get into the habit of using the Word of God to encourage your heart. Rehearse to yourself, "I shall not die, but live, and declare the works of the LORD. Do not allow your righteous fruit to wither and fall to the ground for wicked to eat. Instead, live according to the biblical principles of righteousness and by every word of the LORD. Declare the mighty acts and the works, he has started in your life. Testify, invite others to hear your story. Strong courageous Saints of God shall not die; they know their deliverance is evident in their faith and walk. Deliverance is painful and necessitates deserting personal interests and creating stronger bounds to resist the attacks from the enemy. It is important to understand, Jesus Christ could have easily turned his back and ignored our cries.

On the contrary, his love entraps us under the shadows of His holy wings. The breath of his nostrils, has delivered and anointed us to dwell under the LORD's shadow do we live. Some, have not learned the advantage held is greater than the weakened bands of the wicked. Thus, they die and perish from lack of knowledge forgetting to apprehend the oracles of God and allowing the principles to be rehearsed in the ear.

To live, we promise to tread cautiously and not be captivated or enslaved by the redundant works of the wicked. By day, the enemy haunts their prey with arrows to kill their ministry, steal their joy, and destroy their purpose. However, the heathen can do no more than what we allow them to do unto our vessels. Until we learn to build components to elevate faith to close gaps of uncertainty; the enemy impatiently waits to wrestle with the weak. They cannot contend with freedom because a remnant lives in bondage, waiting for a way to escape.

Be grateful, Jesus did not give you over to death. Instead, he allowed you too live and tell how you girdled your loins by pulling it all together. His chastisement, strengthened your stance and turning the interest of fear into triumphed victory.

Why sit we here until we die from exhaustion? The LORD confused the enemy and knew Jesus Christ was skipping on the horizon stomping out a path for his people to travel far from the barriers filled with camouflaged sins to provoke his sheep. The oppressors devised schemes to place some wanders in bondage while the Hitties who are marred by internal weaknesses devise vicious attacks to charm and enchant.

Diverse circumstances inflicted by different people who are accustomed to the grips of real iniquity. Some wish they could overtake the children of God. The LORD will not allow the adversary to entangle with the Sheep of His pastures. Why sit we here until we die from the inequality of strength he should have possessed from long before.

Green Promotes Maturity, Life, Renewal, And Faith

Commonly, we associate green with evidence of growth and maturity in plants. Maybe, it signifies to keep moving in the direction of hopes and dreams. A green traffic light is an indication to keep moving forward. Yet, some drivers stop and approach with caution, while others zoom through it without thinking about the unexpected. Would it constitute negligence or carelessness about your life? Every day, we move so fast, trying to accomplish tasks that may be the same duties for the approaching days. Not once, do some stop and proceed with caution. Although there are many quotes symbolically explaining the color "green," how many have we believed?

Wisdom Promotes prosperity in all things. Wisdom provides the best explanation when correlating things of old with perfecting the beginning of new ways. We lose time comparing old lifestyles with a new way; when using a better narrative to testify how things have changed for the best. So often, the carnal-minded believes they are more intelligent than the children of God; because we are so accustomed to thinking "inside" of the box. It is okay to think far beyond what you can see to be realistic. Allow the Holy Ghost to teach patience and learn to wait on Him to give the instructions for prosperity. For at least twenty years, Jacob worked for his father-in-law and profited greatly from Jacob's skills at his labor. When Jacob arrived for departing and going away with his family, God did not allow him to leave empty-handed.

Laban profited from Jacob's fidelity, presence, skills and wanted to keep him near for a while many years. By choice, the unsaved would rather keep you and profit from your gift; but are not willing to serve the "Blesser," or Jesus Christ. For the sake of righteousness, Jesus continues to bless them because of you. As such, they will make an effort and try holding on to you like a superstitious good luck charm. Laban requested from Jacob, "appoint me thy wages, and I will give it. When thinking outside of the normality of money, Jacob used wisdom and asked for livestock. Before Jacob's arrival, Laban had little and has increased since he came. So, Laban took advantage of Jacob's honesty and good nature and tried using it to benefit himself. A common perception thought and used on many Christians.

The world truly believes God's people to be gullible and simple-minded because we have no flavor about how we appear to others. Yes, we are green but not naïve to sinful behaviors. Jesus Christ will not allow his people to be taken advantage of, and the Holy Ghost will prick the heart with awareness.

Laban's proposal was presented with craftiness and later overturned by godly wisdom. The bargain was profitable and gifted Jacob with more livestock than Laban. Jacob's faithfulness garnished him to think on the duties to support his own. Now, the time has come for Jacob to provide for his own house. As a husband and father, Jacob is bound by his duties to care for his own. He did not ask for anything more for his hire. But all the speckled and spotted cattle, and all the brown among the sheep, male goats ring straked and spotted; female goats speckled and spotted.

The selection Jacob made would best identify his hire from Laban's. Therefore, it cannot be accounted for or said Jacob has stolen from his father-in-law. Effectively, the bargain was agreed upon, and Jacob used the time wisely and continued to provide services for Laban. While working, the Lord increased Jacob's flock to surpass Laban's. As a result, Laban was covetous and was not happy for Jacob's blessings. For many years he used Jacob and took advantage of his simplicity for his gain. As the LORD blesses his people, the due diligence of honesty will reflect on the countenance of others they have trusted. Often, we lose sight of the true identity of covetous hearts because we are locked in the common threads of "humility or humbleness." However, it behooves us to learn and rely upon the divine support of the Holy Ghost to lead us into a place of surety and security.

Many unjust men and women do not and do not want to know Jesus Christ. They will do whatever to crush dreams because they could no longer profit or draw from your anointing. Stop being so gullible and naïve to your surroundings and know who is with you to promote good and not take advantage of you. The world will continue to consume every aspect of anointing until you are weak and vulnerable. You do not need to build a relationship with people to get where God wants you. In this life, lean on the LORD and depend on the guidance of the Holy Ghost to help achieve greatness.

"Seasoned Saints", are partakers of the deeper truths of the Gospel and should show compassion on the ignorant and on them that are out of the way because we were also compassed with infirmities. Regardless of the length of servitude in the Gospel, it is not a good reason to look down on the ignorance of our brothers and sisters. We are tasked to bear the infirmities of the weak and push them to prevail in the areas of great adversity.

Advise them to grow up, put off childish ways, and fulfill the newness in Jesus Christ. The Holy Ghost is ready to foster spiritual progress which would profess a stronger foundation. Cling to righteousness, and enquire at the hand of God. Build your trust and confidence to gain a reputable relationship that identifies with the principles of the doctrine of Jesus Christ. The deeper truths of the Gospel is evident in the way behave in the presence of others. Christians are often publicly criticized for their behavior.

Stronger Believers can support the growth of others by explaining the Gospel in plainness of speech to promote understanding for the newbies in Christ. Strong meat is for those who are Spiritually mature and understand the deeper truths of the Gospel and is not attainable by those without understanding.

Overcoming Temptation

We must teach what is good and profitable for the soul to prosper and mature. Provide positive instruction on observing Godliness and comforts of entering into a loving relationship with Jesus Christ. In Him, we have an opportunity to build a fortified bond that cannot be destroyed unless allow by your hand. Jesus Christ endows his sheep with greatness to overcome the enemy's snares and filled our hearts with prevailing attributes designed for his people. Having the "Fear of God" in the heart shows complete surrendering to secure prosperity in the knowledge of "Wisdom and Understanding." With both, we are more than capable of leading others into the realm of obedience by living a life worthy of acceptance by the Holy Ghost because we have learned to feast on the Word of God, which gives us the nutrients needed to stand firm.

We are blessed when we chose to uphold the principles of faith and obedience. Daily, we see different messages on items that serve as phylacteries and contain short scriptures which are used as inspirational sayings and reminders. They help us consider our position or purpose in interacting with the LORD and nudges us to praise Him for his faithfulness. Thus, we are obliged to overcome and attest to the victorious testimonies of strength and courage, improving our growth and maturity in Christianity.

When we first experienced Jesus Christ, it was at the moment when we first received him. The feeling could not compare to anything of natural sense because the experience was spiritual and calm. Thus, as we grew, it was a growth, whereas we began to build up faith, trust, and confidence in every area. We were applying the learned fruit of the Spirit to fasten our relationship with despondency upon His strength and courage. Growth means we have cemented spiritual values in believing in Old and New Testament writings.

Envisioning the battles won, rebellious natures, and witnessing in full context the testimonies of how Jesus has orchestrated victories in personal lives. Many know and have learned of Jesus Christ; but have not devoted their hearts. Learning is accepted when the Word of God abides in the heart, and it helps to overcome the wicked acts of deception and folly. We are to share the commandments, statutes, and judgments of the LORD with others to foster growth and maturity. We must teach the young how to obey the same principles of Godliness and fear the LORD. The young include the new souls in Christ and the younger generations. God has gifted us to share and tell of his good works.

Learning Spiritual Growth and Gaining maturity is learning to perfect you in Jesus Christ. You have to want "CHANGE." If you seek it, the Holy Ghost will work internally for the change to be visible externally. Trying to force change will cause you to err in all your ways. The change will not happen overnight, but trust in the LORD; he will sharpen the countenance of your efforts. He will meet you in the intimacy of praise, worship, and exaltation. As you grow in the knowledge of Holiness, focus on desiring more of Jesus Christ and pursue Him with your heart.

According to the Gospel of Truth, spiritual growth and maturity increase as you learn to observe to do what is right. It is not easy to follow the strictness of the Gospel of Truth. However, it is best to try and live up to the standards outlined in biblical promises. So, love the LORD with all your heart, soul, and with all your might. It is an excellent indication that nothing else matters outside of Him. Experience has taught a valuable lesson that Jesus Christ is the Only True and Faithful God who loves unconditionally. As a result, we hide the word in our hearts to help us not sin and overcome temptation. The Holy Ghost will remind us of the promise and keep us from falling. Abide in Jesus Christ, and he will abide in you.

Green Principles of Spiritual Maturity

Though our speech is filled with the parables of righteousness, how could we profit if we cannot find it in our hearts to love? How could we find an easier way to embrace those continually raining on our parade? Or use hurtful words to inflict public shame and pain? I am sure the list could be extensive. As we think about the numerous times we have suffered at the hands of another, at the same time, we are the ones to go back and apologize for "doing nothing." It sounds a bit sad on our end. Yet, because of who we are and the love in our hearts, it is a stronger desire to please God than man. As such, those same people begin to run over your existence as a human being. As adults, we tend to deal with scarred emotions. However, as a child, we use a painted picture to illustrate the details of life. Some hurtful words which caused public shame were met with a fistfight.

Simple and straight to the point. As a middle and high school student, other students always picked on and embarrassed me. Every day, I dreaded going to school because there were so many other horrors of life I was dealing with that I did not have the energy to deal with the bullying, name-calling, and jokes. Since the students made time to make fun and polk at me, I made the time to start the fistfights. It was a way to deal with anger, and fighting was a quick mechanism to eradicate a growing problem. The decision to fight was simple, sweet, and satisfying. Yes, it made me feel a lot better; in my heart, if the student was big enough to embarrass and harass me, then quite naturally, they were ready to dance with these hands. The story is my truth, and it was how I dealt with ignorance.

Being the "victim," in any instance, builds barriers of defiance. No one could break down the walls, so the anger turned to hatred and isolation. When we allow ourselves to get to lowliness filled with oppression, only Jesus Christ can soothe the pain. The transition does not happen overnight because it did not take overnight to build up such a wall.

Somethings come by fasting and praying. These two things can only be performed and implemented after spending much time in the presence of God. In your walk, you do not need friends in ministry to pray with you. From the start, build your relationship in Jesus Christ and allow him to place the right people in your path to increase your maturity in obedience. These people may be newcomers (someone new), whom you never met. So, you build friendship, bonding, and trust for added support. Their hearts are new because they know nothing about you or your past. It brings new meanings to building on a clean foundation and is comparable to a painter using a blank canvas to express new emotions.

By then, we learn to love ourselves and appreciate personal accomplishments. Hopefully, the new friend sharpened your "Spiritual Maturity" without being judgmental but honest and genuine. Based on the interaction and words of encouragement, you will know if they were sent to help you build your faith in the LORD. Sometimes, we have to rearrange the pyramid of friends. It is essential to rearrange your friendship because as you begin to grow in Christ, you don't want to be reminded of past iniquities. Often, old friends love to reminiscence about old habits.

True Believers adhere to new principles and create paths that will lead to prosperity in ministry. As a seed is planted, we expect it to take root, grow and produce. In remarkable similarity, as the "Seed," God's Word is planted in our hearts; we expect it to take root, multiply, and grow. Initially, a sprout is green and has not matured enough to produce its offspring or fruit. However, its transformation will become evident over time because something new will appear on its stem. So likewise, as we continue to grow, there must be evidence of change.

Change is seen in a newborn baby. It transitions from the womb and then through adulthood. The physicians carefully observe its developmental stages to ensure it receives the proper nourishment for continued growth. If a problem occurs, the physicians will acknowledge the disability and try to correct it medically.

We must continue to grow in uniqueness and become distinguished in our physical appearance and behavior. Learning to put away childish things and seek good according to Biblical principles. Transitioning from sinner to Saint is to say, "I no longer want to be identified as a lost child." On the contrary, there is a desire to want more, and willingness can help determine the outcome of strength and courage. Learning obedience requires studying the Gospel of Truth and allowing the Holy Ghost to plant seeds of righteousness in the heart.

What is in the heart will reflect on the outside by behavior. "Green" indicates vivid truths, hope, and healthiness. So, it is essential to generate good fruit and not behave unseemly in awkwardness. Many Christians struggle with their place in the Body of Christ because they are not sure of their worthiness to accomplish greatness. So, they remain in the same position, not willing to go any further in ministry. Let's look at things in this manner, if a tree remains green and never shows signs of maturity, how would anyone be made aware of its change. It must produce fruit or budding flowers to indicate change. Otherwise, it will be seen as a healthy green tree, suitable for shade.

Rejoice in who you are in Jesus Christ and rejoice in your truth. Obedience is better than any sacrifice we can give or offer to The Lord as we learn to obey the commandments of God, than we can love and show charity to others. Afterward, the Holy Ghost will open our understanding and share with us increments of wisdom entailing the pain and brokenness of all those that have hurt us in the past. They find weaker vessels to inflict with shame to hide their insecurities and fragmented relationships. In life, we have all experienced some blunt trauma in relationships and cried without shame.

As a young lady, I did not understand the effects of brokenness until I began to mature in the commandments of God. As the Holy Ghost taught, I fell often and got up with skinned knees and filthy garments. The difference is that I never gave up on maturing in every area of my life. Regardless of the duration, I wanted to grow deeper in Jesus Christ, and progressing in "SALVATION" is painful.

Before meeting Jesus Christ, we were dirty, wretched souls. Accepting him as LORD and Savior required purging, sanctifying, and removing impurities. In other words, it is one-on-one with The Holy Ghost. Maturity is different for every Christian; you, a friend, can not help you build your relationship with Jesus Christ. From the moment of repentance and acceptance, you established a transforming partnership from sinner to Sainthood. Now, the properties of your fruit are not to produce corruptible fruit.

On the contrary, as a "Saint," the verifiable properties of your fruit are the "Fruit of the Spirit." As we Spiritually Mature, our life changes to reflect new beliefs that align with seeking out good actions. The Gospel of Truth inspires a different attitude and leads in a direction opposite of desiring the secular acts of wickedness. Life is full of mysteries, and if we are not careful, much of it is designed to chain us to perish because our hearts lack charity and introduce the prosperity of envy.

Green principles are defined scriptural and are deeply rooted as we apply ourselves to studying. Creating healthy relationships means rendering our life. Altogether, we agree to transition to living God's way, performing duties, and maturing in wisdom, knowledge, and understanding. Our faith helps determine the stance, forcing us to examine the level of trust placed in Jesus Christ. We are like green trees depending on the Word of God to provide the nutrients for growth. Faith in the principles of God should not leave room for doubt or disbelief.

By faith, at the acceptance of Salvation, our hearts believed in the redemption power that "The Blood of Jesus" cleanses us from all sins. Moreover, the green principles of Spiritual Maturity help shape our dependence on the "Holy Ghost" and its ability to fulfill and oversee our faith as we struggle for change. It reminds us, "Faith is the substance of things hoped for, the evidence of things not seen." When change is not visible, others will believe we have faultered in our walk. So, we must grip the principles of righteousness and obedience to support our walk in Jesus Christ.

The green principles of Spiritual Maturity start with the promises of God, which are factual and accurate. These principles must be anchored in the heart and exercised in our life. Thinking positive, believing you have the power to strive beyond opposition and failure. Get acquainted and delight yourself in the LORD. Allow the Holy Ghost to reveal understanding in God's purpose and will for you.

Green Branches Bring Forth Much Fruit

Solid and devoted Believers remain steadfast in the commandments of the LORD. However, when the heart's overwhelmed by life, Christians lose focus and swerve from the laws of righteousness. With ease, their mouths recite the promises of God, but they are double-minded, wavering in disbelief. Questioning your walk-in Christianity when you continue to struggle in your flesh is alarming. Possibly, your heart is not aligned with the perpetual truths of sanctification. The foundation is not as solid and unstable and causes you to disconnect from the vine. Fiery trials and tribulations should encourage growth toward holiness and produce good fruit that can profit the Kingdom of God.

If not grounded in biblical principles, strength is weakened by complaints, which is a proven indication of a dry branch. Disconnecting from the vine causes severe damage, which is repairable by repentance and forgiveness. Many hearts wax cold and die because they lack the nourishment of the True and Living Vine, Jesus Christ. Unripe grapes are shaken off because they refuse to grow on the vine. As flowers connected to an olive tree, we are to produce much holy and not corruptible fruit. Jesus Christ will shake off his flower as the olive because it is not multiplying as commanded.

A branch cannot be effectively mature when it is abiding by iniquity. The wicked deeds of lascivious desires devour it. Strong green branches are not quickly burned because they are full of water and protect them from fire. Jesus Christ is the water abiding in the branch. As such, the branch remains stable and is not easily persuaded by fiery trials and tribulations. Take account of your present state of mind or wellbeing. The Holy Ghost has provided wise instruction to produce fruitfulness because the richness of God's Word invites Spiritual Maturity.

A green branch brings forth much fruit, and the blossoming flowers are evidence of its accountability in Jesus Christ. He allows it to be blessed in size and appearance. On the outside, it looks healthy, vibrant, and alive on fallow grounds and is not bothered by the adverse effects of unforeseen circumstances. Regardless of the storm, a green branch will continue to abide in the vine, giving it the strength to stand as a strong, able-bodied Saint.

However, a dried-out branch is hollow and fragile. It has not retained the commandments of God and has broken away from the biblical principles of righteousness. It lives according to personal habits, which has weakened its growth which caused it to lose its flowers. Dried branches cannot withstand fiery uncultivated situations and die by the adverse effects of transgressions and sins.

A dried branch is unskillful because it returned to darkness. The uproar of calamity has frightened it and later oppresses its heart with the world's disparities. A green branch does not desire to remain close-knitted to the world's vanity because it's filled with torment and deceit. Worldliness has nothing to offer a green branch that is set and created to survive raging storms. Nevertheless, we have an advantage over the world. Our advantage is "Jesus Christ." So long as we continue to acquaint ourselves with learning all which is excellent and profitable to the soul, we will continue to grow. Do not be moved by unforeseen circumstances. Instead, remain faithful in your salvation and strive to be a green branch bringing forth much fruit by increasing within the prosperity of the Holy Ghost.

What Color Are Your Leaves

2 Corinthians 5:17-19; John 4:24; Genesis 6; Genesis 7; Revelations 1:5; Psalm 23:5; Isaiah 58:14; 2 Timothy 2:21; 1 Corinthians 6:17-20; Genesis 8:11; Hebrews 2:17; 2 Corinthians 5:18; Romans 5:10; Colossians 1:20–21; Philippians 3:12–14; 2 Peter 3:9; Romans 7: 1,21; John 15; Galatians 5; Philippians 2:12; Proverbs 3:8; Psalm 52:8; Psalm 92:12; 1 Peter 1:23-25; Psalm 33; Acts 9:5; Acts 26:14; Psalm 119; Deuteronomy 32:12-13; Proverbs 10:22; Psalm 104:16; Luke 9:23; Psalm 1; St. John 7:37-39; Ezekiel 17:24; Isaiah 1:29-30

The Stages of Spiritual Growth

Make Up Your Mind

Salvation takes a lot of work and commitment to obey and follow Biblical principles written in The Bible. It does not matter if you are reading the New International Version, A Study Bible, King James Version, or any translation whose teachings are about The Godhead, Trinity, or in simple everyday terms, The Father (God), His Son (Jesus), and The Holy Spirit. I am old school, and you will see words like The Holy Ghost, referencing "The Holy Spirit." It does not matter how often you read, pray, or study. What is most important is that you do something to break up the fallow grounds of your heart. For many years, we have fallen short of the Glory of God and, without reasoning prefer to live as "stiff-necked" or stubborn human beings, always thinking and taking the easy route through life. Unfortunately, there comes a time when we must make up our minds and choose to live as righteous or unrighteous people.

"The Church" has been crucified by popular opinion for all the wrong reasons. In Church, so many are fighting to find their purpose in God. While searching for their identity, many remain broken and unsatisfied with themselves. As such, newcomers bump into such people and are hurt by their actions. Church hurt is predictable, but others in The Church will give support as we journey together in Holiness. The mission of Salvation is never about how long a person has been in Church. On the contrary, it is about when they believed and started building their relationship with Jesus Christ. It is never an easy task; the most challenging part is choosing what is necessary to start planting, growing, and developing into a Tree of Righteousness.

The Preparation Stage Clearing the Ground

In Genesis, God caused a flood throughout Earth because it became corrupt and was filled with chaos in His sight. The seeds planted on earth were to flourish. Instead, their sins caused them to perish as wickedness prevailed extensively, and disobedience angered God. He condemned the first harvest and replenished it with righteous seeds to restore righteousness.

It was not God's plan to destroy humanity. On the contrary, the wickedness exemplified by humanity remained the root cause for uprooting a bad harvest filled with sin. Restoration is a necessary process and a requirement for starting over. Accepting Jesus Christ is admitting that your old habits and life were unpleasant.

The spiritual man is renewed by uprooting the natural man and sinful its sinful nature. We do this by becoming born again, not of corruptible but incorruptible seed. The flesh is like grass, unstable, and cannot defend or maintain the transition as an incorruptible seed. The corruptible seeds planted the sinful nature manifested into works of the flesh which are adultery, fornication, uncleanness, lasciviousness, idolatry, witchcraft, hatred, variance, emulations, wrath, strife, seditions, heresies, envyings, murders, drunkenness, and revellings. The characters or behaviors connected to sinful nature will not inherit the kingdom of God. These things are part of the natural man, which Jesus Christ removes before laying a new foundation. Mixing bad and good seeds will cause spiritual warfare.

As such, Saints cannot live a double life pretending to serve God but tiptoeing to play in the dark. Truthfully, God is an all-seeing God looking from heaven; he sees all the sons of men. Secondly, is it worth playing double jeopardy with your life? We cannot manipulate The Lord. It is hard to kick against the pricks because at the end, we find ourselves in a defeated position whereas Jesus Christ will always win. Newness is creating new paths never traveled. Desiring it means that the old no longer has lost its value as there are feelings of emptiness. The soul is drowning in silence; starving for substances that provide satisfaction and fullness. Fruitfulness regenerates the spirit giving it the boost it needs to be fresh and alive.

It will not be easy to disentangle yourself from the carnal nature. Our faith will suffer if we try planting on top of old habits. It is best to forget everything behind; otherwise, it will stunt your growth. Deny yourself, and do not let iniquities separate you further from serving The Lord. Instead, allow Him to purify you through Himself and through the Gospel of Truth. The preparation stage started when you accepted Salvation. You were "Born Again" with incorruptible seeds. The Word of God can take root and begin to flourish deep in the inward parts of the Soul.

So, allow the heart to receive the incorruptible seed being the Word of God as it will give power to persevere in the face of adversity. The cleansing process is a time of vulnerability. It is detrimental to take heed of Biblical promises and apply them in your day-to-day life. The transforming power of God's Word will manifest to create renewed hearts and a righteous spirit that will penetrate your Faith by adding the foundation it needs to build deeper trust in The Lord. We want our faith to transform in the Glory of God and not wither away. Nurture and strengthen your faith in The Lord by trusting He can more than cleanse and make you whole in Him.

Change Is Not Easy

Change is an inevitable and necessary process. The Gospel of Truth is life-changing and shields His people when they hide the Word in their hearts. It strengthens your connection to the Vine, Jesus Christ. If you choose not to change and remain still, you will be unable to grow properly in the Spirit and slowly die due to malnourishment. As a result, you desire a change that would restart, restore, and redefine who you are in Jesus Christ.

It is never easy to turn away from the human nature of sinful habits. The Body of Christ has diverse people from all walks of life. Still, they are considered "ONE," filled with unity and love. The Body of Christ is not about race, creed, or ethnicity. Salvation is not prejudiced as it is offered to everyone to partake in Servanthood.

Simply put, a new Believer's heart is transitioned when accepting Jesus Christ as Lord and Savior. They become new in Christ, old things, such as their old life and habits, are no longer remembered, and they start all things new in Jesus Christ. The relationship between "The Father, Son, and Holy Spirit" is Spiritual and not carnal. The transition from old to new is "Spiritual," meaning the Holy Spirit will help you discern between good and bad habits. Moreover, God is a Spirit, and all

True Believers, whether new or seasoned, must worship him in spirit and in truth. It is not a one-time act of obedience, but an everyday practice of worshipping total submission to The Lord.

The Planting Stage Begins with God

Spiritual maturity is understanding the targeted image you desire to mimic; hopefully it is the character of Jesus Christ. After salvation, we seek to develop wisdom, knowledge, and understanding of a sacrificial lifestyle. To achieve spiritual growth, it is essential to participate in Church scheduled services by way of attendance. As we remain committed, devoted, and determined to draw closer to God, spiritual maturity changes with progress. We are striving to attain perfection by following Jesus Christ. Our faith has allowed us to apprehend all that is learned in depth and in all manner of workmanship. Spiritual Maturity is achievable by letting go of old habits and sinful deeds. Continue moving forward and press toward the mark for the prize of God in Christ Jesus.

The color of your leaf depends on your faith and work. Also, it can symbolize Growth or Weakening; both are determined by the planter's or gardener's attentiveness to caring for it. A process that requires commitment, devotion, and determination. We can always expect God to uphold His promises to His people. Unfortunately, only a remnant will strive to obey in total submission. True Believers undoubtedly trust and love Jesus Christ regardless of the trial or tribulation. They understand that commitment, devotion, and determination are required for growth and maturity in servanthood. Salvation has beneficial and essential requirements for the Body of Christ that promotes development in every aspect of life. Living is being "ALIVE IN THE THINGS OF GOD." Vessels of Honor transition to Men and Women of Valor with the power, strength, and authority to withstand secular hardships and not abandon Holiness.

As growth takes on its changes, you, as the fruit, must be willing to trust the husbandmen to plow and nurture your inner man according to his Authority and Power. The husbandmen know exactly what nutrients are needed to enhance and boost your identity in a new place filled with Mercy, Grace, and Truth. "What Color Are Your Leaves" is a parable that allows the Believer to self-check their progress after accepting Jesus Christ as Lord and Savior. A self-check is simple as 1-2 and 3.

Take the time to analyze the number of times you have practiced:

> Kneeling, Sitting, or Lying in the presence of God to pray and talk with him.
> Reverence and Worship
> Reading and Studying the Bible for at least one hour
> Attending Church for Bible Study (Opportunity to learn and gain knowledge).
> Attending Regular Sunday Service

The list is not extensive, but essential to Spiritual growth and maturity and is a small step toward changing behavioral and old habits. Participating in prayer, worship, and Church activities is a personal growth expectation that supports the building stones needed to create a solid foundation and relationship with Jesus Christ.

Forget about the rhetoric from others for babbling noise haters should not have a barren on what you are doing to sustain a solid relationship with The Church and in the Spirit. At times, you will be confronted in Church by others that are jealous or envious of your growth. If you can, ignore the attitudes and keep it moving. Do not allow the actions of one or two people to discourage or jeopardize your course in serving The Lord.

What Color Are Your Leaves? In gardening, we understand that brown leaves signify that the plant is experiencing undergrowth and needs water, plant food, or some type of nutrient to boost its growth. If something is not corrected, the plant will quickly die. A personal Gardner will look for a solution to save the plant because they care about it growing and maturing into something beautiful. Likewise, Jesus Christ is concerned with our growth towards holiness and transitioning to an ambassador or fulfilling a vocation in The Body of Christ. If we are continuously working, building, and trusting in The Lord, he will keep His promise, having patience, and it is not His will that anyone should perish. Daily, it is imperative that we walk in the "Mode of

Repentance." Our hearts and minds are not always in sync with The Holy Spirit. The affairs of this world cause wayward battles to take place without notice. Even when the mind is set on doing what is good, evil is always present to test the foundation, knowledge, and Salvation.

> "The Lord is not slack concerning his promise, as some men count slackness; but is longsuffering to us-ward, not willing that any should perish, but that all should come to repentance.

Desiring To Do Good

Trying to sustain healthy leaves is to depart from impurities and toxins that pollute the nutrients. Such additives uproot and weaken the "Spiritual" foundation you are trying to build. There is a law that is waring in your spirit. Your carnal mind, which is "human nature," is warring against your "Spiritual mind," which is obedience and righteousness. Here you are trying to do what is right in the presence of God. From the beginning, it seems everything is attacking you, your home, job, children, and the list can go on. Possibly, these mishaps were already present; but have worsened. Here, a "New Believer" would say, "Man, as soon as I got SAVED, things are not getting better but worse." Well, The LORD knew such things would test the character of His people. For this cause, Apostle Paul wrote to the Romans, "I find then a law, that, when I would do good, evil is present with me."

Those of us who know the Law of Righteousness understand that it will control our life as long as we live. We are committed to serving Jesus Christ, devoted to the Biblical Principles, and Determined to obey righteousness. We understand from experience that the world has nothing to offer; but struggles, fiery trials, and tribulations. These things will not cease while serving Jesus Christ. However, we are equipped with the tools for spiritual warfare and have a Commander and Chief who has never lost a battle.

While building, The Holy Ghost teaches you how to maneuver and strategize against the oppressor. Afflictions are challenges to your FAITH, and turning back on your SALVATION is not the correct answer. As long as the Branch (you) remain connected to the Vine (Jesus), you will receive the nutrients to grow strong and bring forth good unto God, which are the "Fruit of the Spirit," according to the Holy Ghost.

The Growth Process Depends On the Connection

In order to flourish, the branch must remain connected in the vine. We are seeds of Righteousness planted here on Earth to multiply in wisdom, knowledge, and understanding. The years a person has been SAVED does not exempt them from any scriptures. God's requirements are not altered and is written for wise instruction for His People to follow. The title "Christian" is abused by so many, including the backslider and hypocrites. I do not refer to myself as a Christian but as a True Believer who follows the Laws of Jesus Christ as written and established. If you acknowledge and say you are a "Christian," please do so without hesitation. Most important is to harmonize in the Unity as Bible Believing followers with the concepts of Holy Scripture.

Jesus is the true vine and His Father "God," is the husbandman. Although Jesus died on the Cross for our sins giving himself as the propitiation for wretched souls; He humbles himself before His Father. Today, some family values are destroyed by the adverse actions of children revolting against the parent(s). Many have lost respect and, in some instances, refuse to humble themselves before their parents. Jesus Christ humbly references himself as the true vine. He came as the Word made of flesh, lived, and walked on the earth. The Father planted His Son in the vineyard, which is earth, to serve as the vine to heal, deliver, save, and set free. The Vine grew, spreading throughout the land to the ends of the earth. As Jesus Christ worked in the vineyard, He acknowledged and honored His Father. Likewise, as we grow in the Spirit of God, we must recognize Jesus Christ in everything we do. The fruitfulness or maturity in service is due to His Excellency; as the true vine, he enriched his people with spontaneous strength and courage to stand tall without withering. Every branch abiding in Him that does not produce good fruit; will be taken away.

When you notice your slothfulness in servanthood, it is not too late to repent and keep moving. Trust me, every Child of the King knows when they are not putting forth their best. Remember when you were in school, and sometimes you would slack off and not study, and your actions were evident in your grades? Either you search for a solution to improve your grades in the upcoming grading period or just fail. The consequences were retention or drop-out.

Salvation is the same—as attending your courses to pass and achieve greatness in The Body of Christ. A Saint that is not producing and maturing will slowly fade into darkness and despair. Hence, they will begin feeling sorrowful for their actions, hiding from other Saints because they feel embarrassed. Listen, many Saints have fallen, repented, gotten up, fallen, repented, and gotten up until they finally decided to follow Jesus Christ wholeheartedly.

He takes unfruitful branches away if there is no evidence of maturity. Let us visualize a tree planted in the yard. A branch has fallen, is barely connected to the tree, and is slowly drying out. Eventually, the branch is cut down and discarded because it no longer resembles a strong branch. Moreover, no other small branches or leaves are sprouting on its surface. While we as branches are connected to the vine, we are taken away if we do not bear or resemble some of the fruit of the Spirit: love, joy, peace, longsuffering, gentleness, goodness, faith, Meekness, and temperance.

Against such fruit, there is no law. No one can condemn you for having green leaves and bearing such fruit, which is good nurturing for others. During moments of weakness or falling into diverse temptations; do not stop building your relationship or stop your vocation. Acknowledge, confess the sin to Jesus Christ. Your Salvation is no one's business. Your behavior should be the same in or out of the presence of the Lord. At Church, there are some folk who puts on a show, leave, and go home with empty hearts. They did not take heed to the message or Biblical teachings.

Everyman must work out their own salvation with fear and trembling. There is no better way than repentance with a sincere heart. Jesus Christ can work with a willing heart that is producing fruit. He purges it by cleaning, cutting, pruning, and separating the branch from weeds. Bad company and habits choke the Laws of Righteousness out of the heart. As a result, your repentance brings more fruit; because you are committed, devoted, and determined to live an acceptable and pleasing life to Jesus Christ. Therefore, the branch must remain connected to the vine and increase in good fruit production.

Going to scheduled Church services helps clean the Soul through the spoken word. The Word gives life and sheds light in places of darkness. Often, people receive restoration power to move forward in life. Do not become self-righteous or blinded by your own understanding. Instead, fear the Lord, and depart from wickedness that attracts deception. I will be healing the navel and marrow to the bones. A healthy branch produces bright, vividly green leaves that appearing healthy in their relationship and position in the Body of Christ. Rember to abide in Jesus Christ because you cannot bear fruit; without Him, you cannot do nothing. No other god or source can elevate or promote your Spiritual Maturity except you abide in the vine which is Jesus Christ.

As the Gardner, Jesus Christ allows change to take place on the inside and makes it visible to the naked eye on the outside. It is the "Divine Interpretation and Representation of His relationship with his seed. When a seed is placed in the ground, it is covered with soil and watered. If the process goes well, you will see it sprout in about a week. Change has taken its place inside, and its growth is visible outside.

The Watering Process

Our progress in Holiness becomes visible depending on Commitment, Devotion, and Determination. The first day of acceptance of Jesus Christ was a choice to prepare the heart for uprooting and replanting. Before a farmer starts a new harvest, the soil and ground are tilled to create good soil for seeding. As such, there is a "Preparation Stage" to secure a firm foundation.

Overflow

While partaking in Church services, you will hear a word like "overflow." It means being Spiritually saturated in the Blood, Anointing, Grace, Mercy, and other holy attributes. In the washing away of sins, Jesus loved us and washed us from our sins in his own blood. Sins are forgiven, and we become new creatures or human beings. Also, through total commitment, devotion, and determination putting forth the work to maintain your Salvation is the preparation for God's protection against the oppressor. In His Sovereignty, the Lord anoints your head with oil, my cup, which is your Temple or Vessel to run over.

Planting Vessels

Vessel of Honor

Separate from dishonor and receive honor from The Lord. Purging, cleansing, or removing from ungodly habits makes us vessels of honor. We have chosen sanctification, which is met for the master's use. Denying ourselves the pleasures of the world is preparing unto every good work pleasing to the Kingdom of God. Serve and call on the Lord out of a pure heart. A vessel honor is ready to overflow in the anointing of God.

Temple of The Holy Ghost

Secondly, we are joined unto the Lord as one spirit. Therefore, starting new means to flee the corruptible seeds of unrighteousness by putting away every sin committed against our bodies. Jesus Christ is the owner of our body as it is the temple of the Holy Ghost, which resides in the Soul; and belongs to God. We do not own ourselves; Jesus Christ paid the price. Therefore, glorify God in your body and spirit. Our entire existence belongs to God.

Jesus Christ serves as the benefactor in providing everything to secure the life of all his people regarding the body and soul. He prepares the table in abundance to satisfy the hunger and thirst for righteousness. According to the measure of Faith, our cup runs over in God. He allows us to delight ourselves in His Word, which provides plentiful provisions and guidance to higher places in holiness. Hence, the LORD will comfort and manifest himself in the mind and thoughts of his people. However, we must meditate and enjoy serving with commitment, devotion, and determination. Growth becomes evident through the work performed. As the head is anointed with oil, it serves as a Covenant as God being our God, and we are His people. As such, we desire to build an alliance with God. Our human nature is carnal and cannot serve God. Surrendering gives total access to spiritual blessings and the ornament of delight. Jesus Christ has prepared for our continued growth in Him. Let us get to work and start planting Seeds of Righteousness.

Spirit of Reconciliation

The "Spirit of Reconciliation" is working to reconcile the soul back to God, who has reconciled us to Himself by Jesus Christ. After the Flood, the Dove bringing back an "Olive Leaf" represents "Reconciliation" and the "Height of Newness." The process for Reconciliation is the effect of total Commitment to the Commandments of God, Devotion to seeking His Presence, and Determination to live Sanctified and Holy. Since our relationship is restored back to the Father, He no longer holds our sins against us. Through confession of our sins, Jesus saved us with His life and granted us the ministry of reconciliation.

The old life made us His enemy condemned to misery and pain. With a loud voice, we proclaim the Gospel of Truth and seek perfection as the Blood of Jesus Christ has made atonement for sins. Cleaning us from all unrighteousness through faith in Jesus Christ, Our Lord, and Savior. By faith, we are justified towards righteousness. He has made us ambassadors to share with others the "good news" that they can receive the ministry of reconciliation by turning their hearts back to God. We must prepare our hearts and minds to sustain the good nutrients provided throughout the Word of God. A healthy relationship sprouts forth, bearing strong green branches as we remain connected to the true vine in Jesus Christ. After experiencing turbulence in life, God allows for a break to rejuvenate and replenish. Sometimes, a break from ministry is plausible due to ailments or unforeseen circumstances.

However, it does not excuse us from retaining a prayerful life combined with worship and praise. It is okay to find balance between Church and Personal family affairs. Whatever might be the reason for the short break, always return and continue rebuilding. The planting Stage began at the beginning of the process with The Father, Son, and Holy Ghost. As such, the Trinity, not the Church, determines your development and strength. Take the time to self-check from the day you accept Jesus Christ to this moment. Have you started flourishing, thriving, growing, and prospering in your relationship with "The Father, Son, and Holy Ghost? The growth process determines whether your leaves are green or brown. Do not give up. Keep striving and pushing against perilous times.

The Power Decreed in Green Trees

Be An Olive Tree

Consider yourself as a green olive tree in the house of God and trust in the mercy of God for ever and ever. An olive tree adapts to its temperatures and handles transitioning through elements quite well. Although, Saints endure many changes in life, it is important to adapt to fiery situations by standing firmly anchored in Jesus Christ. Pickup the attribute of resilients and weather the storms without wavering in your faith. Even when you have fallen, your faith should have generated such Trust and Confidence in Jesus Christ that you can bounce back without shame. Such a behavior comes with knowing who you are and understanding The God that you serve. SALVATION is real; but remember it is Jesus Christ the strengthened your stance in Him. Strong Saints will not look like what they have been through when confronted with turbulence. The Glory of God erases the scars the naked eye cannot see. It becomes visible through your stories and testimonies.

Palm Trees

Attracts because its neutral appearance adapts and encourages others when confronted with turmoil. You flourish in righteousness like the palm trees. Their evergreen leaves endure the most challenging storm and are not easily broken. Anchor yourself in the Word of God and learn to adapt to changing conditions or circumstances. Despite the hardness of the trial or tribulation, build incredible resilience and trust The Lord God as your strength. He will make your feet like hinds feet to keep your heart and mind in the way of his commandments. Your faith and confidence will give you the power to surpass troubles and above your enemies. Do not bend, break, or sway under pressure. Instead, adapt in the capacity of your faith as you can tolerate the atmospheric tensions and the elements of oppression. Breathe the fresh anointing of God's Glory, gain strength, and remain obedient to what is truthful and honest.

Cedar Trees in Lebanon

In your human perfections and spiritual stature flourish in the merit of God's favor. The longevity of your faith, belief, and relationship has anchored your feet in God. Because of your identity and one-on-one experience prove you are noble without a doubt. You trust against the odds, believe when other cannot see their deliverance, and because your faith is resilient and never deteriorate. The hardness of life has fortified your belief as it adapts to changing circumstances. You are built strong, solid, and ready for use in every vocation. You are a tree of many talents, aromatic with the sweet smell of God's anointing and evergreen. Spread your leaves from side to side and cover the inexperience of others. Stand tall as an ornament of God's grace and mercy. The Gospel of Truth is inscribed on the table of your heart; as you have gained recognition, power, and authority to represent the Most High, whose name is Jesus Christ.

Planted by God

The Lord provides the proper nutrients to help His people grow in the wilderness and in uncultivated rough terrains. He will lead his people through without a strange god with him. God is God, and besides Him, there is no other. To understand his Greatness, we must experience and believe He will continue to provide sufficiency in everything to bring us through. Whatever the case, the blessing of the Lord will continue to flow, making us rich in all spiritual things and adding no sorrow. Jesus will continue making provisions to ensure we increase in patience and favor. We do not have to complain but be happy because He can bring his people out of the adversary's strongholds. His Sovereignty is everlasting, protecting and bestowing the fruitfulness of honor and grace upon us. Jesus Christ has planted his trees on the earth to provide fresh water to all that thirst for righteousness. We delight ourselves in following his commandments and rest in the comforts of his word and Spirit. Our Lord and Savior make glad the heart of His people because we trust in Him for all things, great and small. Our leaves will be forever green as we remain committed, devoted, and determined to abide in the Law of Righteousness.

The Dried Oak Tree

Brown Leaves Fade and Wither

Giving up on God is not a good decision, and sometimes life hits hard and knocks us down. Commitment is to apply yourself to complete an obligation. In this case, you made a choice to serve God. Although there are questionable moments, they still try to move forward. If you choose to go back into a world filled with emptiness, it will laugh at your calamities and misfortunes. As a result, you will be ashamed of the oaks or type of tree you desire. A tree that is unproductive and ineffective in its Faith in The Lord. We suffer the consequences and are confounded by the gardens that we have chosen. Gardens filled with weeds, unkept, and overgrown with polluted composites decaying the foundation.

Slowly, you resemble an oak whose leaf fades because its isolated and not connected to its primary source for growth and prosperity. Why desire to fade and wither away like a garden without water? Laying a solid foundation depends on our richness in Faith and deepness of the roots in the Gospel of Truth. Jesus Christ is the Living Water that quenches the Spiritual Thirst, giving renewal and hope. Maturity is to seek after Jesus Christ and search for Him until He is found. Desperation is a call to say, "I refuse to wither, dry out, or crumble in the hand of "OPPRESSION."

Jesus is our strength in times of despair; keep following Jesus Christ by denying yourself, take up your cross daily, and follow Him. Give yourself the boost it needs by finding the well of water deep within your soul. Delight yourself in the law of the LORD and meditate on His Word in the day and night. It will provide the fresh anointing needed to sustain your growth in him. Over time, your roots will go deeper into the foundation of your faith, like a tree planted by the rivers of water because it is connected to its primary source. If you thirst for righteousness, seek Jesus and drink of the Holy Spirit. Trust Him and believe in the Scriptures; out of your belly will flow rivers of living water. He will send forth abundant grace to cover and keep you from falling. His people are known by the fruit they produce in the Holy

Spirit. If you remain connected, Jesus Christ will continue filling your belly with comfort and peace; to help you through the dry seasons. A holy life is better than a life filled with unrighteousness and sinful deeds. In Jesus Christ, whatever you do will prosper, and your leaves will not fade or wither away. In due season, you will develop in the Holy Spirit and exhibit fruit that resembles the fruit of the Spirit.

Miracle Growth – Element of Surprise

An idiomatic saying, "To attack the enemy with the element of surprise," uses the Holy Spirit's power to help stand firm in the face of adversity. However, we must be persistent in all areas of invocation to pray and intercede for yourself and others, Supplications making your requests known to God, Conversations is regularly talking to the Lord, Meditations is quietly sitting and reading the Bible, Sanctification is separating yourself from all unrighteousness, and lastly, let the Holy Ghost complete the entire operation.

God Will Restore

Every Saint of God will experience some type of situation because none are exempt. However, it is how we deal with our problems without losing our Salvation. All trees planted, whether small or great, know God's power and authority. High trees are brought down, low trees are elevated, and green trees experience drought. The tree that was thought to be lost through life tensions, afflictions, and conflicts, Jesus brought to life, and it abundantly flourished.

A word spoken by God can fulfill the deepest void. Never give up praying for souls we think have turned their back on God. Whatever might be the reason, there is a break that needs love and nurturing in desperation. We have to love and care for one another because we never know when we might be the tree in the field that the Lord repositions in unpleasant situations. God has the power to restore the branch that may seem to fade but is deep within as thriving and green with faith as small as a mustard seed. In times of trouble, the roots remained committed to serving God, devoted to his commandments, and determined to live and not die. Remain near the river's side, and receive righteous nourishment because seeds planted in water activate and accelerate their growth. The Color of Your Leaves depends on you remaining committed, devoted, and determined.

Green Makes the World Go Round

Anyone can wear green, that's the thing! You do not have to be unique and live high in the sky. It is as simple as pie as its color moves from side to side. Green represents many things and is keen to change. Change for the good or changes for the better or change for the best. It is really up to you—your decision to grow out of curiosity into the realm of knowing what is beyond your basic understanding. Go ahead! Jump up high and try reaching the sky. If you keep trying, one day, you will fly. Fly like the wind, as it says hello, bumping into your skin. It greets you with the ambition of strength and courage, symbolizing the tomorrows of persistence and never giving in. Why would you give in when green makes the world go round? You are running circles around the circumstances which tried pinning you down to the ground. But you sprung up and tricked them by surprise.

They didn't see your growth from the changing seasons of despair to fair praises and things similar to happiness. Do you know what I mean jellybean? You danced in a circle so fast with those new shoes on your feet. No one knew it was you because their hearts were green with envy. Somebody hated seeing your growth because it means they are part of the cloud of witnesses that surrounding your victory dance.

Green makes the world go round! They are sad because many wanted to see you doing bad. Lost is a great word, and defeat is even worse. But guess what—you sprung forth like a new flower in a dry garden. Or maybe like one of those weeds we see shooting out from rocky soil, and inquiring minds wants to know, "how!" How were you able to grow when you were stuck between a rock and a hard place?

Huh—they look confused, scratching their heads, trying to figure out how you got away. You escaped the grips of shame and were raised far beyond the fame of poverty and stuff like that. Green makes the world go round as it rotates and rocks back and forth from the sin it contains. You made one of those quick football moves and dodged the fiery darts of the enemy. It was a shuffle to the left and more to the right. They were not ready for the motion of the promotion. Many hearts waxed cold, from the young and old. Someone pretended to be a "good friend," hoping you would let them in. Let them in on the secret of your success. The sinner will not believe Jesus Christ will bless their repenting hearts. They believe they are too far gone, down in the dumps, nowhere to be found, a castaway, sitting like ugly ducklings without a pond.

Green makes the world go round! In the realm of holiness, coldness does not have a place. Warming hearts matures the soul to think beyond the frantic strings of chaos and confusion. Those friends around the corner are wondering why you are no longer entangled with complex issues garnished with ignorance. You have sprung forth like a watermelon seed, covered in dry dirt, from the drought of anguish. No longer are you cracking with violent outbursts fueled by a rebellious nature. In a Summer breeze, you found shade under one of those trees far off in a corner with a bit of green grass spread at the bottom of the tree trunk. There you lay, using your hands as a pillow behind your head, with a twig sticking out the side of your mouth. Relaxation at its best! Free from worries, the grinding of bickering arguments, or empty patterns without shapes. You have sprung forth like a tiny flower budding from the armpit of a tree planted by living waters.

Green makes the world go round. Do you like the way it sounds? It is compared to a tapping melody, filled with La-la-la's and Ha-ha-ha's and merry sounds like those notes and things. You know what I mean, jellybean! Green makes the world go round, and it is up to you. Break up the fallow grounds, seek Jesus Christ, allow him to plant seeds of righteousness amongst thorns and bristles. Shoot forth. Anyone can wear green, that's the thing, do you understand jellybean?

Green, Sunshine!

Green is a vibrant color, vivid in intensity, bold in its destiny, courageous within its personality, and growing tall against atrocities. Don't let the world fool you. It does not have all that you need. How can it encourage growth and nurture love when it never knew love? Its friend is deception; they plan things together to inflict hiccups and trip-ups. Their schemes caused many to fall back into iniquitous habits. Some looked down and around to see what caused them to stumble. Unknowingly, disbelief, anger, wayward thinking, and instability made them captives—imprisoned by blatant desires.

Hum—I almost tripped over my own feet a few times. Our insecurities and search for validation are invisible taunts that clutter our thinking. Mistakes accent downfalls and serve as entertainment for others. Unforgettable moments are retained memories pending usage to "one-day rain on your parade." Yeah, folks do that from time to time. We have the authority to use mishaps for lessons learned. If you think about it, Green—Sunshine introduces ways to grow. Its boldness does not hide. If you give "Change" a chance, it will adapt to its polluted environment. Nothing can stop its maturity; "Change" finds ways to spring forth. Its determination promotes adherence to all things under the sun.

Change has the power to influence the behavior of hearts. Broken relationships find common ground for at least one soul to search for a more positive outcome. Green Sunshine promotes maturity without notice because it adheres to the commandments of God. Remember, change occurred in the Book of Genesis as "God" spoke. Things and Relationships originate from certain beliefs that are plausible and common to knowledge and willing hearts. Different aspects of how we perceive things can determine the favorable outcome if its neutral foundation is identifiable in God.

As the constructor of FAITH, Our Lord and Savior, in His Omnipotent power, serenades us with His Presence—broken links, such as misunderstood words that do not populate with love, form animosity and despair. Green Sunshine deciphers immaturity by searching for the righteous seed amongst the corrupt—the root of piety blossoms into understanding in vivid colors for all to see. Immaturity is an opportunity for God to work in the vineyard of his people's hearts. His workmanship encourages strength in weaknesses by softening the unplowed grounds of the Soul.

Green Sunshine sprouts from the rays of laughter, shielding your emotions from stormy teardrops and angry winds. Run and stand under the Pavilion of Confidence. Tear down barriers of lowliness and stand tall like a tree bowing at the Throne of Grace, waiting for its moment to bloom out from underneath the boulders that held it captive.

Shades of Green against Shades of Blue are Armies fighting to endorse vibrant springs of "I will be and I do." I will speak with determination, and I eagerly search out the contents of its Faith and trust in the Almighty to uphold us with His Right Hand of Righteousness. Green, Sunshine knows the entitlement your name carries as it is pinned upon its person. Everybody can say they know somebody who continues to struggle with personalities that should differ from old lives. There remains a residue of trembling Faith that can stunt imminent growth in happiness. Green, Sunshine forces a Soul to rethink their journey and the direction they wish to take. Paths are led by arrows pointing in different directions, which could lead to desolate places.

Please do not say your former days were better than these days. It makes you appear confused and disoriented in your thinking. Some days will appear cloudy and gloomy for a season. Refiguration of the heart and mind is an unpleasant look and feel. Emotions are in turmoil, and brokenness is visible to the naked eye. Former days are hidden deep in the shadows of treachery. Before, we walked in the blindness of our lust as it indulged the corruptive fruits of misery and strife. It is not wise to enquire about the old days. It is to wish one never wanted the gifts from The Blood of Jesus Christ. It is an uncompromising gift you cannot repay, for it is priceless as it brings happiness to wounded Souls defeated by envy and strife.

Don't tighten your fist to war against the flesh, for it thrives in chaotic situations that draw mutiny against the laws of righteousness. How can a closed fist wave show total submission? It yells defeat to the gloomy clouds of disdain and impurities. Release negativity—in the sighs of relief. Let it flow through atmospheric tensions into a realm of tranquility. Green Sunshine provides cool breezes to calm the heart and Soul. Look far beyond the shades of blue and grab the bits and pieces of happiness—a smile here and there will one day transition into a peal of bursting laughter that tickles the Soul. Inward laughter is a slight chuckle as it scrambles to find its way out for all to hear its contagious jolly. Change has a schedule that only the "Great I Am" understands. He commands "Change" to interact in a time and season unknown to Man. So, we sit with Patience, waiting in deep thought, making an effort not to complain, but trusting that The LORD and Savior will send it soon.

Green Sunshine is finding your spot amongst the other Victorious Souls that give God the Praise for Love, Grace, and Mercy. Crowds of True Believers gather around to see them dance to a tune that only listening and receiving hearts can understand. Those hearts don't see Change. However, Patience invited them to a party with singing and dancing. Join the Crowd of True Believers and dance with Love, Grace, and Mercy. Although they do not know when Change will arrive, they still trust that she is on her way. At any given moment, they are expecting her grand entrance without delay. There are aspirations set to encourage the movement of winning. Regardless of how big or small the victory, take your baby steps and receive every success with an openness of heart and stand firm. Green—Sunshine symbolizes Change. She has pulled you from immaturity to maturity in Faith, Trust, and Hope.

You could have left 'Change" before she arrived. Instead, you stood still, waiting on the "Salvation of the LORD." Hence, you witnessed "Change" for the first time. You envisioned her through the Spirituality of your Emotions and ignited Faith. In return, she tapped Trust on the shoulder and whistled for Hope. All things depended on your willingness to sit and wait with Patience. The "Great I Am" caters to willing hearts surrendering to his commandments. Green, Sunshine is an open invitation to work on your appearance using the attributes of Patience, Faith, Trust, and Hope. They can multiply accordingly and answer to the commandment of the Creator.

So, why are they referenced as pronouns "she and her?" Well, I am happy that you asked such an excellent question. Green-Sunshine understands that only women can multiply and produce according to God's Commandments. He refers to Wisdom as "she." Don't you believe me? Hey, I just got the revelations at the beginning of the sentence. Please do not take me to be so deep that I cannot hear the voice of the Holy Ghost speaking. Listen, because I just did! Get your bible and let us turn the pages to *Proverbs 1:20-22 Wisdom crieth without; she uttereth her voice in the streets: She crieth in the chief place of concourse, in the openings of the gates: in the city she uttereth her words, saying, How long, ye simple ones, will ye love simplicity? And the scorners delight in their scorning, and fools hate knowledge?*

Wisdom has been up and working from the beginning. To understand Wisdom, you must receive Instruction, which will help you Perceive the Words of Understanding. This Green Sunshine is attributed to Change, Patience, Faith, Trust, and Hope. Come alive in the vivid colors of happiness and intensify in the boldness of Courage. Change is forever running, trying to make her presence known to all the unbelievers, haters, and gossipers. Her job is not easy, as she makes haste to encourage Souls. She takes pleasure in encouraging others to keep going and believes in their existence in a world filled with atrocities aimed at destroying Patience, Faith, Trust, and Hope.

Green, Sunshine reinforces your position as a Child of The Living King. You are peculiar in more ways than your heart could ever imagine. Without Patience, your eagerness will leave her stranded, and you will never know Blessing. Patience helps to train the heart to wait for the Salvation of the Lord. She encourages "longsuffering," which is waiting for The Lord to secure and send help during troubled times. She quietly whispers, "Wait, I say, On The Lord." Remain attentive, making prayers and supplication in His Name. Trust in the Holy Name of Jesus; He will see you through with great sincerity and secretness of heart.

Green, Sunshine is vivid and filled with boldness. Do not give up on who you are in God. Patience invited you to a party where there is singing and dancing. Join the Crowd of True Believers and dance with Love, Grace, and Mercy; they do not know when Change will arrive, but trust she is on her way.

Greenhouses

Proverbs 4; Jeremiah 20; Psalm 35; Hebrews 11; Proverbs 1;
Deuteronomy 22; 1 Corinthians 15; Exodus 31; Deuteronomy 10;
Proverbs 6; 2 Peter; John 15; Numbers 31; Psalm 91; 1 John 1;
Job 38

Choosing A Structure

Year-round, regardless of life-changing events, devout Saints learn to adapt without altering their Faith. They remain in "season," prepared to go and share the gospel. Our connection to Jesus Christ increases our survival amongst atmospheric tensions when we compromise in unfamiliar settings. Disobedience affects and disrupts the balance between our Faith and living holy. Although we live in this world, we are not part of it. As such, it's in our best interest to survive in the wilderness filled with snares of the enemy.

Many Saints fall prey to strange habits, thus damaging their growth. Full acceptance of Jesus Christ changes inward and outward appearance. So, we strive to survive in predestined elements to darken our journey path. As we mature in our Faith, we are taught to survive against the devil's wiles. Spiritual practices such as fasting, praying, and worship are often tricky to adjust to. However, when we learn their meaning, we will understand the value each has towards our growth in wisdom, knowledge, and understanding.

Greenhouses build their houses on a solid foundation, with an infrastructure strong enough to sustain the elements of struggles of life. The Word of God provides the stable foundation needed to build courage and helps to jump-start our self-confidence. Comparing yourself to the life of another possibly will cause discouragement. So, never look at how others worship the LORD. Instead, find your balance and achieve greatness in your salvation and relationship with Jesus Christ.

Every environment is different, and the atmospheric tensions differ because of the lifestyles. Force yourself to pick up your Bible and read. Try spending at least thirty minutes with the LORD and bridge the gap daily. Understandably, everyone does not like reading. Reading the Word of God invites you to learn about what happened in the beginning and middle and what will occur in the end.

It's a map of how your life started, in the middle of troubles, and what the expected end would tell. Folks tend to stand afar and look for the shortest route to take. Unfortunately, there are no shortcuts in building your relationship with Jesus Christ. There is much work to complete to start with the shedding of the old and applying the new man, a task that can only be completed by the Creator of all things, Jesus Christ.

Building Codes

Greenhouses are built with perfection and according to the spiritual standards of righteousness. We are designed to endure storms that are raging in strength to alter the Faith of the devout Believer. Often, we are confronted with undesirable circumstances and concerned if we have the power to triumph in the wind victoriously. Indeed, our dependence upon the source of our strength will never fail us in the weakest moments of despair. Ears have heard Faith is the substance of things hoped for and the evidence of things not seen.

The (substance) is the fundamental nature or principles of trust in Jesus Christ. As such, it helps to transition our greatest expectation into the expected end we hope to receive from Jesus Christ. Believing beyond doubt and never faltering in the promises are in His majestic powers. We are designed to win against the odds when others expect us to fall—looking towards the Holy Ghost for guidance and strength to stand when the knees are feeble. Regardless of how others may topple at the mire gestures of the brazing wind, you are built to stand firm in the Faith measured and poured into your temple.

Several folks laugh at the Children of God because so many faints at intimidating factors devised by the enemy. Intimidation challenges our perspectives on secular values and substitutes opinions with traditional or faith-based ethics. Others may have heard the old saying, "learn to pick and choose your battles!" Contrary to popular belief, every battle belongs to Jesus Christ. Hence, we are taught to practice "Nay or Yay" and keep moving. Great debates or challenging cultivated issues do not build our Faith in Jesus Christ. The world laughs because some believe the Children of God are ignorant and weak.

Our fundamental nature is etched in the heart by the Holy Ghost. Studying "Biblical Principles" helps build resistance against the devil's wiles. With understanding, we can bridge the gap between ignorance and folly. The Holy Ghost fills our hearts with the Spirit of Wisdom and Discernment to help us apprehend the knowledge of God.

The world's perception towards Christianity is to question the writings and oracles of Jesus Christ. It has deemed our religion unworthy and has worked to tarnish our purpose by speaking false narratives, challenging how we ought to live or carry ourselves. Spiritual blindness has blocked their understanding, leaving them astray in a lonely place. The world has its notion of what Christians look like because of those who continuously straddle the fence. Unfortunately, their description does not define "True Believers." We comprehend with greater wisdom than the oppressors. Undoubtedly, "Nay and Yay" interjects simplicity to lessen secular values short of merit.

Following heated debates is not profitable for "True Believers" because it takes much energy to create a fire that will continue burning the moment you walk away. Thus, it is easier to leave the door shut and allow another to open it to their peril. Your ears are attentive to The Holy Ghost, who transitions thoughts to rest on all things truthful and edifies the Body of Christ. We cannot produce from unreliable sources. Our Faith is the substance of what is expected and yields a good report.

"Now faith" is what we believe is true according to the word of God. Thou there is no proof, we feel complete with our hearts in its entirety, the Biblical writings. No matter the circumstance or what others may perceive. Our "FAITH" is defined by the measure of trust placed in the Omnipotent Power of Jesus Christ. By these words, I continuously rehearse in the ear of the LORD, *"I don't know when, I don't know how, I don't know where; but, I trust Jesus Christ to work it out."*

Many have heard, "Now Faith is the substance of things hoped for, the evidence of things not seen. By it, the elders obtained a good report. Testimonies are spoken and shared throughout generations. True Believers, holdfast to the promises of God, and embrace the scriptures as published.

Fire Shut Up In My Bones

Grab hold of the "Burning Desire," to abide in God's Word! The Holy Ghost burns on the inside of our soul to bring the warmth of God's tender mercies for continued growth in Him. The more we adapt to the newness of Life, He prunes us by cutting away bad habits and imparting treasures that produce "Fruit of the Spirit," reinforcing the foundation in Him. Only Jesus Christ has the power to give his people an ornament of grace as they adhere to his excellent doctrine, forgetting not the laws of righteousness. Then, we will learn how to appreciate her wisdom and role in promoting honor as we retain and keep the "Commandments of God" in our hearts. Whatever the reason for the desired growth, let it be for the enlightenment of the Church and not for personal gain.

Heavenly gifts secure the hands for service in the House of God. He is adding diverse talents and willing hearts to encourage growth, igniting God's Word in the heart as a burning fire shut up in the bones. The faithfulness of Jesus Christ inspires the weariest soul to trust without restraints and believe He is a Keeper of his promises. Take time to reflect on his name and make known His love. Developing strong branches and staying connected to the Vine requires a specialized "Love," which only flows from Jesus Christ. He cares so much for his people that the Holy Ghost was given for support while lighting the way through tempestuous trials and ensuring a deliverance as a testimony for the Glory of God.

No one can keep quiet when they have learned to endure hardships without breaking the Covenant laws of righteousness. Their hearts will not allow them not to mention the Savior of their soul. Instead, they yelled his name from the rooftops, and high mountains echoed the majestic powers of Jesus Christ and how he delivered them from despair with a loud voice.

Greenhouses produce elements designed to destroy their purpose. But, we have learned to take hold of shield and buckler and allow The Lord to stand up for our help. It is impossible to bring forth fruit without the Word of God nourishing the soul. The LORD knew us while we were in our mother's womb. As we grew and heard of His Greatness, hearts turned away from wickedness and searched for the hand of God. When we made the first step to return, Jesus Christ started renovating and building a "Greenhouse" to withstand the elements of the world.

We must allow The Holy Ghost to take complete control of every aspect of our life during the process. As we continue to grow, our hearts desire more Spiritual and less fleshly attributes, the secular values filled with old habits. Give yourself enough time to grow, never letting go of the commandments of God as taught from the time you knew and heard of him. Invest in your relationship with the LORD. Ask him for whatever heavenly talents you desire to enlighten your understanding.

Attached

Greenhouses are vessels that are filled with the anointing of Jesus Christ. Because they understand what He means to them. Without a doubt, their Faith remains devout and solid. They are creating fortified walls which are sturdy while remaining attached to the source of its growth.

Stay connected to the vine! Live in the Presence of Jesus Christ and desire to be filled with His Glory. Spiritual Fruit cannot produce in your life if you have disconnected from the source of Salvation. Jesus Christ establishes our foundation, ensuring a solid structure to withstand diverse storms. Life has its way of inviting itself as it brings unfavorable circumstances which try the building materials. Without Jesus Christ, choosing imitation materials to establish your foundation will buckle against brutal winds. We forfeit the right to secure "The Holy Ghost," which enables power to stand. The branch cannot produce fruit without its primary source unless it remains in the vine.

Sometimes, trials and tribulations are heated to the core, which causes hearts to shift in their faith. Weak houses fall under pressure, backsliding into old habits and disconnecting from the Vine. Not abiding or remaining in Jesus Christ electing not to live according to the Laws of Righteousness is disobedience. Any soul not willing to walk upright is a castaway branch that withers. A vessel no longer fit to serve is thrown in the fire to be reformed and restored. Complex trials are not designed to break us but teach hard lessons that direct us back to Jesus Christ. If we could understand such a thing, we can indeed receive chastisement for our sins. Going through the fire purifies the heart and enlightens our understanding that Jesus Christ will not forsake us to bear such a heavy burden.

Although hearts wax cold and shift from serving Him, Jesus Christ is always near to forgive and love. The fire of "The Holy Ghost" etches the anointing, strength, and eternal power on the tables of the heart as it inscribes the commandments. A sincere heart will acknowledge the principles of obedience and turn back to their "First Love," Jesus Christ. The morals of their guilt no longer control their existence amongst the unbelievers. Recognizing weaknesses giving them over to the Creator to restore brings about restitution. When we delight ourselves in the Laws of Righteousness, oppression is dethroned and uprooted by repentance.

Walking in holiness requires purification of all areas of our lifestyles. Whatever is offered to Jesus Christ must be the best. Presenting our body's is to deny ourselves of unwanted pleasures. We can endure hardship like good soldiers with the Holy Ghost as our Shield and Protector. We are trusting Jesus Christ to sanctify and baptize us for reasonable services. Abide in the secret place of the Most High and abide under the shadow of the Almighty. While you are there, take time to reflect on the current situation and elect to serve a Living God who can sustain and protect you from the elements of destruction. Obedience brings forth deliverance. A clean willing heart can bear good fruit.

Keep in mind that the yoke was destroyed because of the anointing. You can rise far above the circumstance because Jesus Christ fully delivered by removing the burdens of tyranny and sin. His redeeming power has reconciled us back to The Father. As such, we can now reconnect, abide in the vine, and continue to grow as partakers of the anointing of Jesus Christ.

Have you heard someone say, "Attached by a strain," to be hanging onto the beliefs of power and hope barely? We hope to excel, wish to change, expect to be blessed, hope to do so much farther beyond doing our best. To achieve such a change, abiding in the vine is to press on even when you do not perform at your best. Trusting in Jesus Christ against the odds brings great Glory and Honor. It conquers doubting emotions and prevails when the heart least expects it. Remaining attached to the vine is walking straight ahead, believing The LORD to guide the steps.

A greenhouse cannot uphold itself without laying a solid foundation to support its growth. Weak materials will cause it to collapse when faced with adversities. Allowing Jesus Christ to lead the building; by all means, he will elevate your power, increase faith, give a double portion of anointing to sustain and protect against infestation that eats away at the core of Biblical values.

Infestations are lustful flesh acts that continuously war against the inner man. Some of us, not all—want to live in a clean house. As such, we do what is necessary to ensure the home is well kept, neat, and not cluttered with excess. Actions are taken to restore brightness if it appears cluttered, dark, and gloomy. The renovating can include many things, but the work must be done to achieve the new look. On the other hand, a few by choice are not keen on dwelling in a clean home. They settle for the clutter, darkness, and gloomy atmosphere.

Whatever you desire to be in your relationship with Jesus Christ, the work must be performed. He is not of darkness, but the "LIGHT," As adopted Sons and Daughters, we must partake in the holiness. We walk in the light, as he is in the light, we have fellowship one with another, and the blood of Jesus Christ; "Son of the Living God," cleanses us from all sin. Fastening ourselves to Him is surrendering to the Biblical principles of righteousness.

The LORD laid the foundation of the Earth, measured it, marked the Equator, and laid the four corners North, South, East, and West. Why not allow The LORD to lay a foundation which will promote spiritual growth and maturity? The Holy Ghost will show all things and guide our laboring in it. We cannot strive for greatness lingering with disgraceful shame. Iniquity eats at the root, killing the seed before it develops. Without the proper care, Seeds of Righteousness will not have a chance to mature. The Fruit of the Spirit will not produce because the greenhouse is not willing to maintain its structure.

Salvation is FREE—however, we must diligently work to prove that we belong to Our Father. Trials and tribulations teach us to seek more excellent support to pass the subsequent storms. Sometimes, we get comfortable, forgetting that unforeseen circumstances never cease to develop. The enemy will attack unguarded houses. Secured houses lock out the intruders because their fortified walls are designed to withstand unpredictable attacks.

Jesus Christ has given insight into constructing solid houses and has provided the materials. We must use the materials by applying them to support development. The Holy Ghost informs and helps with the work. In times of distress, He will encourage us to trust in the power and strength of The Living and True God. His greatness conquers adversity; nothing can stand against His powerful judgments. Greenhouses are chosen to grow in strength, faith, and courage. We have diverse talents which are produced by and through the Holy Ghost. Let us get to work! Remain attached to "The Vine," so we may grow and bring forth good Fruit for the Body of Christ.

Freestanders

The "I's" who believe they made it to the top of the mountain alone without help. So, they found their place amongst the heathens and have hearts of easy persuasion. Their disconnection impacts growth and development. So many are malnourished because they have detached themselves from holiness into the grips of iniquity. Without the light, their foundation will weaken under the added pressures of life. Worrying about the cares of life entices the weak and causes them to go astray from serving Jesus Christ.

As the wander into desolated places, they begin to wither, dry, and become brittle. When the world has depletes good talents, they destroy the person.Since, they cannot produce any good thing, the prey destroys their character, binding them to shame. Those who knew their good, will pass them by like run-down houses without a builder to care for it. The "Freestander's," emotions are scarred by overwhelming guilt, until it falls into deep depression.

Their hearts are sorrowful, as pride takes to the front against repentance. The path back, is repentance. It extends their growth by reconciling their hearts to Jesus Christ's Creator. For a little while, they stay away until there lives began to fall apart. It is impossible for a freestanding tree to multiply and grow. It cannot do everything alone because it needs help to grow and mature to strengthen its branches.

Freestanders can do nothing alone. The working of the carnal mind will entrap them; sending them into a downward spiral. Do not close yourselves into a dark cave. It will swallow you whole without piety.

Listen for the voice of reasoning and search for positive energetic vibes. Delight yourself in the LORD, and watch him do the impossible.

Distress Signal

Occasionally, we do isolate ourselves from the world to seek after the goodness of Jesus Christ. These "Free-standers" train and isolate themselves from others by detaching and not relying on others to support their growth. Betrayal or bad relationships destroy their trust. They treated others with kindness, loved without restraints, encouraged when hearts were disappointed—only to be hit with betrayal. Caged emotions ignites a distress signal which force an abused heart to isolate, clinging to the elements of loneliness in hopes of preventing further emotional distress. The infinite power of Jesus Christ erases past failures. Collectively, He is willing to abide in the hearts of those who seek to know Him.

Self-Reflection

Periodically, we separate ourselves to build a stronger relationship with the LORD. By doing so, we seek forgiveness, spending time in the presence of God confessing our sins from all unrighteousness. The objective is to examine one's internal feelings and cast life's burdens upon the LORD. Then, evaluate your purpose and perfect your salvation both mentally and spiritually. We were reflecting on hidden faults that caused us to stumble in keeping the commandments of God. All have failed at something and have found ways to overcome the attributes of failure. To achieve victory, personally reflect on self by examining imperfections.

When we set our minds on evaluating ourselves, there will not be enough time to point the finger at another soul. Self-reflection gives enough space to think about your present position in Jesus Christ. How often do you converse through prayer, worship, and praise? These are essential spiritual habits that increase trust in Him. Learning to communicate is an attentive approach to knowing God's voice.

From childhood, we learn to listen to our parents calling our names and vice-versa. Each became accustomed to recognizing the voice and hearkening to the call. If we did not communicate, how would we know who is calling? Placing yourself in the presence of God is to get better acquainted with him. The Father knows the voice of them that diligently seeks his face. Self-Reflection is understanding your flaws and striving to perfect shortcomings. Participating in prayer, praise, and worship takes much diligence and willpower. Prayer allows us to purge negative thoughts and refocus our hearts on encouraging efforts to enhance greater values. Once you learn how to communicate with the LORD through these channels, you will understand the importance of glorification. It brings about peace, gratitude, and love. Occasionally, it is good to separate yourself for a short time. Your mental state should not be focusing on the issues of life. Never get too comfortable being alone because there is strength in numbers.

We can find fulfillment in the Word of God. According to our understanding, the Holy Ghost, our Comforter, inspires our work at a sufficient pace. Self-Reflection also helps structure a "just right" path for you and will work towards the expected end determined by The Gospel. Take control of the anointing and power of The Holy Ghost by allowing it to lead you away from destruction and into a righteous and acceptable life.

Spirit of Discernment

How can we walk upright before the LORD without direction? Adaptation to "doing what is right" profits the soul to gain strength against the enemy. Understanding the "right way" means doing things "God's way." Having the "Spirit of Discernment" provides guidance, helps to judge well, and recognize the authority of God. As you grow into the "Knowledge of Truth," it promotes liberty from the laws of sin, whereas we can serve the LORD in fullness. It will deepen our relationship by governing our behavior to help us walk agreeably in the Spirit. Total devotion emphasizes our ability to stay on the right path with a clear, conscious heart to yield to the authority of God. Commune with Jesus Christ, rest in His Presence, and Love Him unconditionally.

We cannot influence others to follow Christ if we have not gotten ourselves together. We must set aside moments of despair by trusting The LORD to deliver when we least expect it. Nonbelievers observe how we handle life afflictions, whether standing or falling. Whichever comes first, get up and keep moving. Salvation is striving to become "MORE, LIKE JESUS." Stop thinking about current situations, gird yourselves, and start building. Know that the love of God is real. He will not leave you alone to battle the adversities of life. Keep the lines of communication open by making your supplications known to Jesus Christ.

Choosing What to Produce
Corrupt or Spiritual Fruit

Some of us were not fortunate to experience a childhood, where Jesus Christ remained the core value. Some of us had broken parents who neglected their responsibilities. Possibly, their parents did not experience or have the privilege to grow up in a home where "Jesus Christ" was its foundation. Nope, some of us were drawn by the preachings and teachings. When I accepted Jesus Christ, people respected the Bishops and Founders of the Church. The old path is covered, and a new approach is made to resemble worldly practices unacceptable to Jesus Christ. "The Old Path," to the modernized Christian, has lost its salt, and seasoned saints are viewed as stubborn. As such, when modernized Churches hear the melodies rising from "The Old Path," hearts are pricked by fading words of wisdom.

A soul can learn a variety of gifts by seeking the old path and allowing the Holy Ghost to plant seeds of righteousness. Every soul can choose what to grow and produce in their greenhouses. Salvation is freely offered; however, you must work to maintain your willingness to grow. We have the liberty to live free or remain bound to the laws of the oppressor. The Holy Ghost has diverse talents to give. Growth and development begin in the House of God. In his house, the wise will hear, increase in learning, and a man of understanding will attain wise counsels.

Either way, a "Greenhouse" can choose to uphold the Laws of Righteousness, reaching its full potential in the King's house. Firmly adhering to the instructions, not drawn away by uncertainty or lingering suggestions. Harmful atmospheric elements can damage the roots, causing the foundation to decay. When the foundation is unstable, the damaged areas of life can affect others.

Do Not Sow with Diverse Seeds

By liberty, we can choose what we want to do in the Kingdom of God. Our choices could strongly impact growth and development in and out of the House of God. As Children of God, we must NOT LOOK THE PART, but—live and lead a lifestyle that mimics Holiness.

Work in the field which you are ordained to fulfill. Stop trying to imitate others because you chance losing power and anointing. Often, we try so hard to be someone else without fully understanding their struggles or the blessing received for their level of faith and workmanship. It is easier to plant seeds familiar with the aspects of commissioned offices, such as doing what you are called to do and perfecting the "Calling" or "Ministry" before trying new assignments. Greenhouses must focus on their current position by completing it and then wait for The Holy Ghost to increase their talent. Jesus Christ fills us with His Spirit, giving us wisdom, understanding, and knowledge in all workmanship to perform the Ministry we are commissioned to operate.

When too much is going on—confusion will uproot happiness by reverting it into disappointment. Emotions will begin to run rapidly high because we have overstepped the boundaries of decency and order. Allow the LORD to give the assigned task to you. Operate in the Holy Ghost by allowing Him to lead, and you follow. Many times, we miss the mark because of selfish desires and impatience. Stop planting different seeds and wait for your current talent to be Spiritually Mature. Then, in due season, Jesus will harvest the talent according to His Will. Children of God should not invite different seeds in their vineyards. Do not allow others to corrupt seeds to sow in your ministry. Their hearts will transition to jealousy and envy as they witness your growth and development. Corrupt seeds produce wickedness relative to deeds of the flesh. Their choice of seed is to crowd your house (vineyard) with weeds to block continued growth. These changes invade praise, worship, prayer, and other heavenly practices.

Your heart will wonder why it cannot reach its peak in its relationship with The Holy Ghost. Unwanted activities associated with the "old lifestyle" will creep back into the "new life" if we are unprepared and ready to uproot weeds. Weeds are people who continuously disrupt your ability to reach the height of perfection in Holiness. They consume every aspect of "YOU," desperately trying to strip off the expressions of God's favor from your life.

Allowing diverse seeds to crowd your branch will produce a cluster of sour talents that are not fitting for the edification of the Church. Disobedience is resisting the Gospel of Truth and committing idolatry with strange gods. Its betrayal to Jesus Christ in the highest degree. Sadly, we return with nothing more to offer than a repenting heart when all else fails. Jesus Christ leads us out of unrighteousness by cleansing us with His precious blood. His love removes filthy garments, which crushes our self-esteem in the Gospel. God's precepts support growth, making us wiser and more conscientious of His plans. Greenhouses are built to stand firm against the wicked elements of the world. God's love teaches us compassion, but it does not mean to be ignorant of our duties.

We are to fear the LORD, walk in all his ways, and love and serve him with all our heart and soul. Also, keeping the commandments is wise concerning all promises written and spoken. His precepts are the necessary nutrients that support growth in strength and courage. If we despise the sayings, we cause tension and friction between ourselves and The Holy Ghost. It is rejecting what is good and acceptable. Disobedience produces forwardness in the heart, devising mischievous behavior continually and sows discord. The fault is within ourselves when this happens because we took our eyes off the prize. Interacting with people who do not desire to know or follow God's plan will cause the feeble to conform to their ways. Their corrupt roots will lead hearts astray, causing many to disconnect from the True Vine. Slowly, the lost will fade into a desolate place, putting themselves back into darkness. Going backward does not equate to fruitfulness.

On the contrary, the work completed is a vanity that deteriorates because it lacks its Creator's infinite wisdom and nourishment. Simplicity confuses the hearts of many because they believe in keeping corruption in their circle. If we expect the seeds to grow in a garden, we put in much work by pulling up the weeds and imparting good nutrients to the soil. We carefully monitor their growth as the seeds grow, breaking through the soil. Moreover, we prune, cut away the brown leaves, and make sure nothing blocks the sunlight.

We can monitor our growth by disassociating with weeds, letting go of unnecessary habits, and following Jesus Christ, the Light of Our Salvation. Unbelievers will not walk according to the commandments of God because they do not know him. When we changed partners, we accepted Jesus Christ, made Him Our God, and became His people. Mingling with seeds (servants) of corruption cannot promise you freedom. They speak deception, and broken promises are devised like a web of lies that pushes you back into bondage.

Instead of showing happiness and characterizing an excellent report, your personality changes like the wind. Be not deceived; evil communications corrupt good manners. Plant seeds of righteousness and allow them to help you grow in wisdom. Malicious communications are not receptive to positive thinking. Their ears are prepared to decipher the opposing narratives of deceit and iniquity. Corrupt seeds produce corrupt fruit and cannot build but destroy. They are weeds that defile clay houses, causing breaks between the crevices and the surface. Be mindful and wise of the people you choose to live in your camp.

Churchgoers are those who desire to do nothing more. However, they challenge the growth and ministry of others. They are known as "artificial seeds" appearing in sheep clothing. They are prey amongst the House of God, a den of thieves waiting to devour the "Fruit of the Spirit." There are clusters of them, dehydrated and void of understanding. Stubbornness prevents their hearts from returning to the Living Water, Jesus Christ. Brokenness has dismantled the strength needed to connect to the Vine. Churchgoers are those who do not desire to develop Spiritually. They are wild artificial seeds lingering in Egypt, bound to a life of oppression.

In return, they have learned to oppress the Ministry of others by intercepting growth and ceasing the harvest. Trying to survive mischievous deeds sown by corruption requires much work, repentance, and willingness to be separated from such a group. Greenhouses must be careful of what is planted. Every fruit produced does not mean it will yield a good return. The Fruit of the Spirit is produced by seeds of righteousness, which is good for the continued growth in the Body of Christ.

Genuine and Refurbished

Proverbs 30:12; Romans 7:6; Psalms 119:59

Trading Stones

Apportioning talents or gifts in areas impacted by life's turmoils provides ways of escape for all whose faith is weakened by unfavorable circumstances. Trading stones does not mean you are trading your gifts for something better or new. Instead, it is promoting support to others whom the adversary traumatically hits. These are broken souls whose faith in God is tainted by the corruptible fruit of fleshly desires. When people are deeply hurt, they walk away bruised and beaten. Honest "Servants of God" humble themselves and serve by trading places with other precious stones which cannot relate or apply personal experiences. Testimonies provide insight while diligently searching through fasting and praying. As the soul seeks the right way, emerging not as a victim; but victorious. They are standing tall and thankful for deliverance. There are different ways to tackle or approach the issue, which we can begin by lifting one another and offering ways to improve, build or sharpen our tactics by sharing words of wisdom.

Edification

Improve, Tutor, and Give Instruction to increased Learning

The more we learn how to do things or accomplish achievements; we tend to stick with what works best. When we started on our Christian journey, we had no idea what to do or expect. So, we learned by failing in every aspect and perfecting our strengths to remain stronger while struggling with continued weaknesses. No matter how many times we have faltered, the most crucial part is staying connected to the Branch, Jesus Christ. Abiding in him garnishes a fulfillment in wisdom, continued knowledge, and understanding. Hence, being attentive, leaning towards the avenues of God's commandments helped us to move forward in Ministry.

The Holy Ghost advances and perfects Ministries to draw and introduce others to share in the unity of Holiness. Sometimes, Christians are so deep that they lose focus on what is required. We should perform and seek out more than one mission! There are lost souls or people who are hungering and thirsting to hear "good encouragement." Kind words can shift atmospheric tensions by removing negative thoughts and replacing them with positive energy that inspires, uplifts, and motivates. Encouragement will remain etched in the hearts and minds of all seeking to build a relationship with God.

So, edification helps to improve the spiritual lifestyle of others. Many of us learned from past mistakes and struggled with endurance while seeking the Gospel of Truth. So, why not share stories to help others excel in their maturity towards greener pastures? Having a person's back in Ministry shows strength and great love. It tells the story of someone who has experienced failure and continues struggling with their imperfections. However, the flaws are not in control, but the overcomer has gained momentum because of their increased praise and faith in the "Great I AM!" You might believe "Holiness and Sanctification" is a walk in the park, huh?

Well, it is more like understanding who and whose you are. You are a child of a King, living in poverty, poorness of spirit, but rich in Grace and Mercy. The best part is acknowledging that you are broken and allowing Jesus Christ to fix everything about you. Listen, there are no magic potions or hocus pocus to help streamline your growth in Jesus Christ. It is putting forth your faith and working out your soul's salvation with and in Jesus Christ. Stop feeling bad about all the mistakes made and move forward in peace.

REPENT, ACCEPT JESUS CHRIST AS LORD AND SAVIOR; then get to work. If you encounter a Christian who says they are without flaws, remove yourself far from them. Because as long as we are in this place we call home (Earth), something or someone can quickly change the countenance of our face. Troubles are prevalent and running rapidly. However, learning to focus more on the things of God and his ability to rectify any issue helps to move forward.

Moreover, find your pace and walk with Jesus Christ. The Holy Ghost will guide you in all truths and provide instructions for improving growth and learning to stand tall and strong like the trees in Lebanon. Be attentive to the Holy Ghost for your eagerness to attain spiritual gifts. He will help you excel so that you can help put your hands towards building and educating the Church. Folk are eager to receive the gifts of the Holy Ghost but are afraid to work in Ministry.

As expected, they are afraid. But, you know, it is not the ministry work; it is the PEOPLE you must deal with both in and outside the Church. Like the world, diverse personalities are channeled from one Ministry to another. Learning to love the "people" is another subject altogether. However, a word to the "WISE," love them, and do not allow negativity to overshadow your growth. Let the Love of God flow against the odds of humiliation and disparity. The jealousy and envy at heart will learn to love you in God's timing. Always think of things to happen in God's timing and not when you expect things to happen. What's going to be—will be, and only Jesus Christ, the Son of the Living God, can change the outcome.

Sharpening

Breaking down old barriers and building new

Let me say this, "When Jesus Christ perfects you, nothing else matters." In other words, there will come a time when you will be comfortable with who you are in Jesus Christ. Hence, we gain knowledge through the Holy Ghost. Its purpose is to instruct on completing the assignment and succeeding against the odds. No flesh and blood can dictate your future. Only Jesus Christ has the divine power to promote and demote. Once it is understood, you have the wisdom to sharpen the intelligence and mindset of another.

Envy and jealousy will always flow rapidly from one end of the earth to the other in this life. However, the Saints of God have greater power to overcome various devious tactics devised by workers of iniquity. Disobedience hinders our growth, which causes many ministries not to flourish. So, when the time approaches to perform, we might falter. Sin diminishes and brings us to open shame. Hence, the adversary has the advantage and wreaks havoc against our prosperity. So then, the weaker vessels fall prey as their talents are sifted like wheat, plundering through the precious stones.

Know yourself and stand equipped to seize the opportunity for greatness in The LORD. Make provisions by producing righteous fruit to sharpen the skills of others, breaking down old habits, and building new habits to shine the countenance of a broken stone. Every Emerald stone has value and deserves to shine bright. Allow the Holy Ghost to transform shades of blue into greener elements suitable for maturity in the Gospel of Truth.

You see when you are not entirely equipped with the power of God, you will become subject to the world and its practices. As such, they look upon the shame, laughing at the despondency of your understanding. Broken and oppressed, the heart is unarmed, tainted by the spears of anguish. A vessel without power is cast before the enemy, looking for a traded stone of courage to sharpen their hope and faith in Jesus Christ. Disobedience carries penalties; however, it is an opportunity for an experienced "Emerald Stone" to exercise their trade in the perplexing tensions of unbelief. As we learn, we gain knowledge, wisdom, and understanding "to do our best and move forward."

On the other hand, if we do not have proper instructions, we are stuck in the garrisons of desolate disbelief, feeling hopeless and faint. The world is rich in working the mysteries of peril because of secular knowledge. The Saints of God are privileged and craftier in all works of life. For this reason, there are "Trading Stones," furnished with heavenly weapons to pull down strongholds and establish weapons of warfare by praying, fasting, praising, and believing the promises of God. Experienced Emeralds are equipped to promote growth when life's battles dispirit broken hearts in others.

Sharing words of Wisdom

We share words of wisdom to encourage the hearts of all experiencing or facing life difficulties. Giving hope helps to delight their hearts in the LORD by showing a different perspective. When a person is offered various ways to view a situation, it broadens the knowledge of understanding. Also, it pushes others to move forward with courage, strength, and power. The Holy Ghost has equipped us with spiritual amenities to strengthen our stance and help support our balance in spiritual warfare. Emeralds are awakened by the beauties lying beneath the levels of disparities. Shame is translucent and appears on the shoulders as heavy burdens and wavering faith. We have endured the heat of flaming tongues wreaking havoc on the self-esteem of the vulnerable.

Far beyond the chaos, Emeralds learned how to come out of the fire with dignity and without shame. The Holy Ghost strengthened our hearts and engraved them with humbleness, obedience, and sacrificial praises. The traumatic experiences burn like fire, causing many hearts to turn from their first love, Jesus Christ, the Son of the Living God. The fire softens the heart, molding it into existence as it yields to its Creator. We cannot "win" without obeying the commandments of God.

We are aware that the struggles of life can distort our faith. However, the effect should be temporary with minor damage. Though our faith appears bruised, we should continue moving in a positive direction. Yes, the struggles of life are weary and burdensome. It has caused some to resist the goodness of Jesus Christ, fearing his love might appear temporary. However, if bruised hearts do not recognize the love of God, they will continuously miss out on their happiness. Thus, we must share wisdom to teach others how to survive life's pitfalls. The LORD has much more to offer than the world. The root of the problem is failing to recognize the "Truth and Love of God."

As such, the Holy Ghost took charge and showed us how to stand against the wiles of the devil. We cry because our days seem cloudy and often appear gloomy. Amid the gloom, the Holy Ghost allowed us to see and feel the tranquility of peace we thought was so far away. Then we realized the importance of depending on Jesus Christ when we felt weak in the knees, unable to stand. The Holy Ghost gave us the support to lean upon the promises of God and to continue to trust when we didn't see a way out. As a result, the disparities and untruths developed false lies. The blunt force of family deceit, dishonest friendship, and a host of broken relationships impacts our survival skills. So, we must desire to overcome and reach toward the positive aspirations of Jesus Christ.

Emeralds resemble blue and green hues, representing the struggles and development towards Spiritual Maturity. So, through the courses of Divine Intervention, we have learned how to endure the strange adverse tactics designed to flaw our beauty. Trading stones is trading unearthed pebbles into Emeralds to take their place on the top shelf above life's scrutinizing shameful pits. Sharing words of wisdom is taking our testimonies and rehearsing the oracles of God in the ears of the deaf. Although they have ears, many do not hear what the LORD says and fall prey to the adversary.

We are bound by the promises of God to support and love our brethren. When we encounter or see others stumbling in their faith, help them over the edge of the wall to escape tyranny. Sometimes, people need a little boost to help them achieve greatness. It is okay to share a word along your journey. When we gained knowledge, "someone" shared with us their testimony, and we listened to them and made it through. The commandments, statutes, and judgments are given to teach and obey so that we will know how to possess the wealth of knowledge needed to exceed far beyond the perils of life.

The commandments are taught with great diligence as inscriptions of God's faithfulness towards His people. He has brought us through the overwhelming trends of follies and given us greater to build. Emeralds are unique and diverse in their own way. Nothing else can compare to the beauty that God has created. Everyone wants to shine like a diamond. Yet, even diamonds are flawed and cannot escape the rugged edges of deception. The hues of blue hidden deep within an Emerald shine forth and blend within the maturity elements of God's grace and mercy. Emerald stones use their victorious moments by trading wisdom and encouragement to help others overcome their struggles.

They Can't Tell

Psst! —they can't tell! He smoothed the rough edges and tailored the corners to perfection. They won't be able to see the brokenness unless you reveal it!

How could we question the workmanship of the Creator? From the beginning, He knew the path we would choose the things we would do, and never think about the consequences which followed. He knew the reckless mistakes, the secrets we tried to conceal, the hatred hidden in the reigns of the heart, and the wicked acts that fumbled from desperation.

Jesus knew all the angles on growing issues before we could role-play them for the world to see and give their immediate opinions. The Creator knows all about mishaps, missteps, trips, and falls. Like us, he probably laughed at the level of our clumsiness. How could we question the workmanship of the Creator? He delivers us from follies with gentleness and brushes away the embarrassing stains. Society laughs at the failures of others, and gossiping tongues play it like a one-hit song. Full of broken lyrics, of a broken soul, crying and seeking love to rescue it from the claws of piety.

A shattered Emerald, flawed deep within and chipped on the edge. There is a hairline fracture that is not visible to the naked eye! Love has buffed it until it was smooth and invincible. So, it shines without the glare, which constantly obstructs the vision. You can see it through the rays of sunshine reflecting from the smile of joy and happiness. Who made it so possible? Inquiring hearts and nosey people desperately want to know. Not to congratulate for the persistence of success but for the anxiousness to inflict envy. Who can question the workmanship of the Creator? An arrogant person without a plan to live above the shattered pieces of imitation gems pretending to be genuine. Fake stones are perpendicular to the angles of deceit and treachery. They set traps to capture vulnerable hearts and the gullible who follow every wind of doctrine. Thus, the weak are lifted high for a short time and later dropped like tiny stones tossed and forgotten.

Who can find such a tiny stone thrown into a world of chaos and destruction? It is shuffled against the rubble like trash blowing in the wind, waiting to be found and reclaimed again. Who would want such a rugged stone? It has lost its shine and no longer looks appealing. It turned, and the reflection from its right angle caught the eye of its Creator. He picked it up, washed it clean, and it shined brighter than before.

What happened to the Emerald that was chipped? It ran off to meet and greet some strange person. It did not know a thing but felt its beauty could bring them popularity and fame. What is a chipped stone good for? It will continue scratching at the surface of freedom but cannot reach its promised destiny. The world has whispered lies in its ear, for the beauty reflected the chipped image of occasional sin, which gained its unknown popularity. The world will take everything from everyone—long as everyone carries their part. There is a price to pay to mingle with the elite, and the return on investment is more than expected. How could we question the workmanship of the Creator? What is the issue? There is no price he cannot redeem. Silver and gold have no value in the Blood of Jesus Christ. His Blood has redemption power that eliminates the return of investment the world desires from broken stones.

When a stone is lost, it never has to worry about being found. Its owner will find it once it stops running from the things it cannot change. Sometimes, we miss out on the most basic things in life because we forget our purpose. When we stop to think about our actions, we can sit still to be found by The LORD. Swift feet never keep still because it desire to keep moving in the direction of nowhere.

Where are you going, and how do you plan to get there? Where is an open-ended one-word statement, "Where?" Uncertainty blocks the avenue for wisdom, and it leaves us thinking. Where will I go from here? It will keep you on a circle that continues to circle empty thoughts.

Know where you are going because not knowing leads to spiral changes. Emerald stones are simple but accent everyone in their inner circle. Green Emeralds are vivid, full of life, and sensitive. The LORD has taught us to stand firm, remain calm, and be sensitive to His voice.

Everyone wants to be a diamond that is glitzy and much desired. Emeralds, go with the flow, smooth sailing, and soaring on the wings of the Holy Ghost.

You know exactly where you are going. So, pick yourself up by walking according to the Biblical principles of righteousness. Moments of loneliness will sometimes arise. Thus, learn how to overcome its claws. Praise and worship build a momentum of strength and courage. It reminds you of your identity and The Love of God, which continues to surpass the things you will never understand. Smile when it hurts, and cry when you are in pain. It is all good, still okay, but remember He smoothed the rough edges and tailored the corners to perfection. The Love of God covers a multitude of sins. So, when you fall, get up, keep moving, and don't think about the gossip. Instead, think about the God of Righteousness and rise above defeat.

It is you, Emerald!

It is you, Emerald! I saw you afar, quietly sitting alone, crying softly, careful not to let anyone hear you groan. The afflictions are deep, and the wound is visible; however, no one sees it. It is you! I knew it when I saw you quietly sitting alone, dazed and confused. Why stare in disbelief, trying to understand the actions of lost souls who know nothing about love? They would never understand good because all they knew was the uncertainties of the perils of life. You came along to soothe the itching thoughts of sin, which goes unscathed. It is well known because of its capability to entertain the youngest minds. Every day, it invents and presents a new thing for a new soul that has etched its way from the formalities of holiness.

Sin is not a favorite person, but you continue to seek it. While striving for something that knows no good? It receives your kindness to sift you like wheat. It is slowly sifting away the precious stones adorning your soul. Stones of peace, tranquility, happiness, and wisdom slowly fade away into the shadows of forgetfulness.

It is you, Emerald! I saw you afar, frantically running and seeking your first love. Where is he? How can I find him? Did he leave me alone to bear such anguish and defeat? Frantically, thoughts of insecurity kick down the doors of security. The heart overflows with the nick-nacks of life's afflictions picked up by YOU. The annoying pestilence of fear awakens, forcing the soul to hide from the adverse attacks of the enemy.

Emerald, It is you! The Gemologist of all stones dug up you—a precious stone. What happened to your courage? What happened to the mighty valours of honour armed for battles near and far? You have lost the Shield of faith to believe in the God of Battles. What happened to the breastplate of righteousness? You lost it while feasting on the delicacies of the world. It entertained your thoughts and fed your appetite for curiosity.

Emerald, it is you—returning from the rugged elements of filth and shame. I saw you afar, frantically running to catch up to your Creator. The gemologist Jesus Christ is like no other. He has received you with love and kindness.

In your eyes, pureness was perceived as perfected in you. But, you have not learned how to attain it in the fullness of holiness and sanctification. Quickly, you faltered back into the relations of misfortune, unaware of the dangers waiting to swallow you whole. Emerald, Jesus did not wash your heart for you to refill it with filthy particles of dust and shame. Accept the rays of light and allow them to pierce the core of your soul. Be free from the perversive rays of anguish and anxiety. The remnants of occasional sins are hidden in the secretive crevices of your heart. Holding onto old things with no value diminishes the sparkle you wish to portray. Let go of the accented hues of darkness because it cannot absorb the commandments to retain its shine. Neither can it absorb enough power to stand and walk upright in the righteousness of God.

It is you! Never mind the critics, both near and far. You are delivered from the laws of bondage. Come, serve in the newness of Spirit and not the oldness of the latter. Emerald, shine brighter than before! We all have fallen on this journey striving to build a better relationship with our Creator and Father of all living things. We learn how to perfect our shine by depending on the powers and strength that reign in the hand of Jesus Christ. You cannot compare his love with another because it is impeccable and unquestionable.

It is you! Emerald, I saw you afar looking more beautiful than before. You have learned to get acquainted with wisdom and ceased the behavior of imprudence. It was not good to continue faltering in the carnality done under the heavens all the days of our lives. Glorify God in the fullness of his counsel and will. He redeemed you through his blood for the forgiveness of sins according to the riches of his grace. Emerald, where is your faith in the Lord? His love is rich and waxes in greatness to the world's end. In times past, you desired the lusts of your flesh, giving into its temptations and slowly mimicking the nature of children of wrath, disobedient covenant breakers.

It is you, Emerald! I saw you beaming with joy. Your reflection is the beauty of holiness, for you have thought of your ways and turned your feet unto the Testimonies, walking in liberty, praising the God of your Salvation. It is you, Emerald! A priceless stone created by Christ Jesus to do good works. He called you to walk in your faith and shine like the repolished stone you are.

Released November 14, 2018

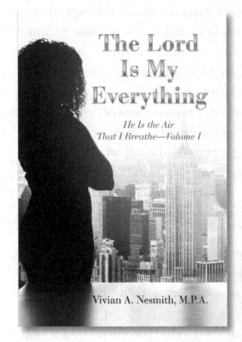

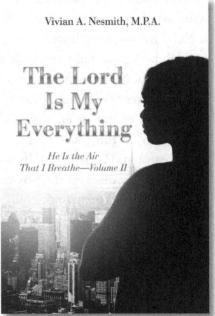

You may purchase book titles on:
https://www.westbowpress.com/en/bookstore
Or Visit My Website:
https://nesmithassociatesincorporated.com/

Released November 10, 2020

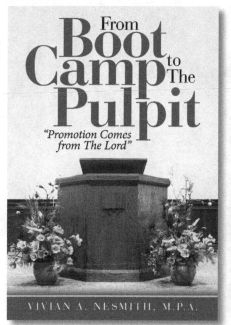

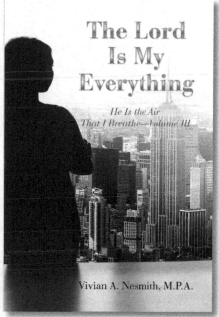

You may purchase book titles on:
https://www.westbowpress.com/en/bookstore
Or Visit My Website:
https://nesmithassociatesincorporated.com/

Printed in the United States
by Baker & Taylor Publisher Services

Printed in the United States
by Baker & Taylor Publisher Services